A PREFACE TO
NEWMAN'S THEOLOGY

BY

Rev. Edmond Darvil Benard, M.A., S.T.D.

MEMBER OF THE FACULTY OF SACRED THEOLOGY
IN THE CATHOLIC UNIVERSITY OF AMERICA
WASHINGTON, D.C.

B. HERDER BOOK CO.
15 & 17 SOUTH BROADWAY, ST. LOUIS 2, MO.
AND
33 QUEEN SQUARE, LONDON, W. C.
1945

NIHIL OBSTAT

Gerard Yelle, p.S.S., S.T.D.

L. Derome, s.P.P., S.T.D., Ph.D., J.C.D.

Censores ad hoc

IMPRIMATUR

✠ *Thomas M. O'Leary, D.D.*

Bishop of Springfield

Springfield, Mass., September 25, 1944

Copyright 1945

B. HERDER BOOK CO.

Vail-Ballou Press, Inc., Binghamton and New York

THIS WORK IS RESPECTFULLY DEDICATED

TO HIS EXCELLENCY,

Most Reverend Thomas M. O'Leary, D.D.,

BISHOP OF SPRINGFIELD

The following abbreviations are used in the foot-
notes:

Newman's works:

Apo., *Apologia Pro Vita Sua*
Dev., *An Essay on the Development of Christian
Doctrine*
Diff., *Difficulties of Anglicans*
G.A., *An Essay in Aid of a Grammar of Assent*
Idea, *The Idea of a University*
Mir., *Two Essays on Biblical and Ecclesiastical Mir-
acles*

Other works:

A.S.S., *Acta Sanctae Sedis*
D.A.F.C., *Dictionnaire apologétique de la foi ca-
tholique*. Paris: Gabriel Beauchesne et Cie., 4th
ed., 1911–22.
D.T.C., *Dictionnaire de théologie catholique*.
Paris: Letouzey et Ané, 1903–39.

INTRODUCTION

CRITICS have been fond of comparing John Henry Newman's literary style, in its apparently effortless lucidity, to a stream of smoothly flowing water with a transparent clarity that is a perfect medium for the contemplation of its depths. Unfortunately, many of the interpreters of Newman's thought have furnished us with an unhappy implicit development of this comparison. Newman's theories and teachings, as presented by some of his professedly friendly commentators, seem to have acquired in the process a strange similarity to the cherished ideas of these commentators. When the critics are unfriendly, they frequently seem to have been prevented by the intruding image of their preconceived opinions from penetrating Newman's thought at all; and they have been quick to dismiss or condemn what they did not entirely comprehend. Newman's style may be, as the commentators say, like a limpid brook. But in gazing into its waters, too many interpreters have seen, as can usually be seen in clear water, a reflection of themselves.

The genius of Newman is many-sided and, like a multi-faceted jewel, reflects a variety of light. We believe that, viewed in its completeness, Newman's thought may be blended, like the colors of the spectrum, into one pure white light, that of a deep and genuine Catholicism. It would be futile, however, to deny that some of Newman's theories, torn from their context and subjected to a dubious interpretation, can be isolated into something like skepticism, or even something close to heresy. It would be useless to deny this, because it has been done. But heretics have done the same kind of thing to the writings of the Fathers of the Church, the Epistles of St. Paul, and even the Gospels. We may be disturbed, then, and annoyed to find Newman thus treated by some of his commentators. We should hardly be surprised.

It is not our purpose to enter into a discussion of Newman as a man of letters. This has been done often, and admirably. We are interested in Newman's religious thought, or, to be a bit more specific, in what we might call his contribution to theology, although Newman was far from being a systematic theologian in the sense in which the Schoolmen understand the term.

As a superb craftsman in the use of the English language, Newman has generally been accorded the high recognition justly his; but the theological thought of the distinguished Cardinal has been and still is the object of wide disagreement. There have been fulsome appreciations like that of Bede Jarrett, O.P., who, mentioning St. Thomas Aquinas, St. Jerome, and the Fathers of the Church, remarks: ". . . for Newman now indeed seems to be of that band and of that stature. The Fathers of the Church were the companions of his musings until he became one with them in fellowship." [1] On the other hand, one of the most widely quoted of the writers about Newman, Charles Sarolea, has a rather different evaluation:

That extraordinary fermentation, which we may observe in the French Church, in the works of Loisy, Dimnet, Laberthonniere, Leroy, Houtin, and against which the present pope has just issued his memorable Encyclical, can be directly traced to the influence of the great Cardinal. The prediction of the Anglo-Roman prelate Talbot, that Newman was the most dangerous man in England, the judgment of Dr. Döllinger that Newman was a heretic, have proved strictly true. [2]

Between these two extremes of white and black, Newman of the "stature" of the Fathers of the Church and Newman the "heretic" and source-author of Modernism, runs a gamut of opinion including ambiguous defenses that are scarcely less derogatory than an outright condemnation. [3]

[1] J. D. Folghera, O.P., *Newman's Apologetic*, English version by Philip Hereford, with an introduction by Bede Jarrett, O.P. (London: Sands and Co., 1928), p. 7. (A translation of Folghera's *Newman Apologiste*. Paris: Editions de la Revue des Jeunes, 1927.)

[2] Charles Sarolea, *Cardinal Newman and His Influence on Religious Life and Thought* (Edinburgh: T. and T. Clark, 1908), pp. 3 f.

[3] Such statements, for example, as that of W. H. Hutton: "But it has of recent years again and again been asserted that he [Newman] was the intellectual parent of a modernism which he would have

It is not unusual that in our own day many Catholics, and even some Catholic theologians, depending
for their knowledge of Newman largely on certain of
his commentators, should find his teaching an object
of vague suspicion. Newman's words to his brethren
of the Oratory when he received the intimation of his
elevation to the cardinalate, "The cloud is lifted from
me forever," [4] reckoned without those misty interpretations of his writings which would do their best to
bring the shadows down again about his head.

No reader of Catholic periodical literature needs to
be told that there has been in recent years a marked
revival of interest in Cardinal Newman—in the high
virtue and serene Catholicism that were so superbly
triumphant over the difficulties and disappointments
of his life. But any such renascence would be incomplete if it were to concentrate solely on Newman's

---

abhorred. A partial study of his writings might give some ground for
such a view; a complete one refutes it. It could, indeed, hardly be held
by anyone who did not, perhaps unconsciously, identify the wider
catholicism of orthodox Christianity with the narrower presentment
of it in modern Roman theology which Newman never set himself
very seriously to defend." Article, "The Oxford Movement" in *The
Cambridge History of English Literature*, edited by Sir A. W. Ward
and A. R. Waller, Vol. XII, The Nineteenth Century I (Cambridge:
University Press, 1932 ed.), p. 270.

We might venture to suggest that Newman, if one may judge from
the whole tenor of his writings, would also have abhorred the lati-
tudinarian application of "catholicism" and the insinuation, contained
in the last sentence, that he would not care to defend seriously the
doctrine that the Catholic Church, Roman and Apostolic, is the one,
true, and only Church established by Jesus Christ.

[4] Wilfrid Ward, *The Life of John Henry Cardinal Newman* (New
York: Longmans, Green and Co., 1912), II, 438.

character and on the events of his life to the exclusion
of the published writings which are his legacy to
Catholic thought. The fact that Newman's writings
have been the target of a criticism often bitterly de-
structive makes it imperative that we re-examine the
whole subject of the interpretation of Newman's
works.

The first part of this study is devoted to the establishment and explanation of certain principles of interpretation which are, we believe, essential to the
determination of the exact meaning, scope, and significance of Newman's teachings. The second part is an
examination, in the light of the principles outlined, of
Newman's theory of the development of Christian
doctrine and of his explanation of the genesis of belief
in the individual, which are generally regarded as his
most important contributions to religious thought. It
is largely because of his writings on these two subjects
that Newman has been accused of hostility to the traditional notion of Catholic dogma, of subjectivism in
his understanding of the nature of faith, and of having
laid the foundations of the Modernist heresy. We hope
that the following pages may play some part, however
small, in helping to dispel the nebulous suspicions,
which still seem to be present in a good many minds,
concerning the orthodoxy of Newman's teachings.

Newman's works, with all their difficulties and, particularly in his earlier writings, their occasional in-

adequacies, should need no elaborate defense. If studied carefully and with attention to their background, they are their own best witness. Cardinal Newman is too often read about, too infrequently read; or at least too infrequently read in the light of those concomitant considerations that so often provide the key to an adequate understanding of his works. This is unfortunate, because for the searcher after truth there is a great fund of spiritual and intellectual enlightenment which the writings of Newman can provide.

E. D. B.

CONTENTS

PAGE

INTRODUCTION vii

PART ONE

THE INTERPRETATION OF NEWMAN'S
THEOLOGICAL THOUGHT

SECTION I

Newman as a Theologian: The Background for
the Principles of Interpretation of His Works

CHAPTER

I. BIOGRAPHICAL NOTES 3

II. NEWMAN'S PLACE AMONG CATHOLIC THE-
OLOGIANS 16

III. THE FOUNDATIONS OF NEWMAN'S RELI-
GIOUS THOUGHT 24

IV. NEWMAN'S THEOLOGICAL METHOD . . 30

V. NEWMAN'S TEMPERAMENT 37

SECTION II

The Principles of Interpretation

VI. THEIR NECESSITY 47

VII. THE FIRST PRINCIPLE 52

VIII. THE SECOND PRINCIPLE 56

CHAPTER   PAGE
IX. THE THIRD PRINCIPLE 64
X. THE FOURTH PRINCIPLE 71
XI. A METHOD OF READING NEWMAN . . . 75

PART TWO

THE DEVELOPMENT OF CHRISTIAN
DOCTRINE AND THE GENESIS
OF BELIEF

SECTION I

Newman's Theory of Development and Its Critics

XII. THE ESSAY ON THE DEVELOPMENT OF
        CHRISTIAN DOCTRINE 83
XIII. THE CRITICISMS FROM CATHOLIC SOURCES 92
        A. THE QUESTION OF TERMINOLOGY 92
        B. THE CRITICISM OF ORESTES BROWN-
            SON 97
XIV. THE CRITICISMS FROM PROTESTANT
        SOURCES 106
XV. NEWMAN'S THEORY OF DEVELOPMENT AND
        MODERNISM 112
        A. THE MODERNIST HERESY . . . 112
        B. THE THEORY OF DEVELOPMENT AND
            ALFRED LOISY 119
        C. THE THEORY OF DEVELOPMENT AND
            GEORGE TYRRELL 128
        D. NEWMAN AND THE MODERNISTS:
            CONCLUSION 151

CONTENTS

SECTION II
Newman's Theory of Belief and Its Critics

CHAPTER   PAGE

XVI. THE ESSAY IN AID OF A GRAMMAR OF ASSENT 157

XVII. THE PRINCIPAL CRITICISM: DOES THE *Grammar* UNDERMINE THE FOUNDATIONS OF OBJECTIVE RELIGIOUS TRUTH? . . 169

XVIII. THE *Grammar of Assent* AND THE MODERNISTS 180

XIX. THE POSITIVE VALUE OF THE *Grammar of Assent* 192

CONCLUSION 200

BIBLIOGRAPHY 205

INDEX 225

PART ONE

The Interpretation of Newman's Theological Thought

SECTION I

Newman as a Theologian: the Background for the Principles of Interpretation of His Works

CHAPTER I

BIOGRAPHICAL NOTES

A CURRENT writer has recently reminded us that any approach to Newman which ignores the peculiarities of his mind or the circumstances in which he lived courts disappointment and bewilderment.[1] This is especially true with regard to his theological works. Newman was always the most personal of writers, and in his every paragraph the reader is acutely aware of the author. In order, then, to understand and appreciate Newman's theological thought, we must know something of the man himself.

[1] Rev. Michael Tynan, "The Approach to Newman" in *The Irish Ecclesiastical Record*, March, 1940, p. 262.

We are interested in Newman's life especially for its evidences of his theological formation, and for the influence of its successive periods on his theological thought. We shall not attempt to catalogue the multitude of events marking a long and active career. Many of these happenings were directly responsible for specific productions among the forty or so volumes that flowed from his prolific pen, and they form an indispensable background for the reading of these works. The student of Newman will, of course, be careful to consider each piece of writing as fitting into its particular position in the framework of Newman's life story. It is to indicate the importance of such a method of reading Newman rather than to furnish all the necessary material for it that this biographical summary is written.

John Henry Newman was born February 21, 1801, in the City of London, the son of John Newman, a banker, whose family seems to have been originally of Cambridgeshire stock, and of Jemima Fourdrinier, of Huguenot descent. He died a cardinal of the Catholic Church at Edgbaston, near Birmingham, on August 11, 1890. He had been received into the Church in October, 1845, a circumstance which divides his life almost exactly into equal parts. The *Essay on the Development of Christian Doctrine*, which he began as an Anglican in the late winter of 1845, and which was still unfinished when he became a Catholic, is a convenient literary and theological link between the two religious periods of his life.

R. W. Church, the Anglican Dean of St. Paul's and Newman's lifelong friend, has given us his impression of the successive phases of the Cardinal's religious progress:

> For it seems that, at starting, he is at once intolerant, even to harshness, to the Roman Church, and tolerant, though not sympathetic, to the English; then the parts are reversed, and he is intolerant to the English and tolerant to the Roman; and then, at last, when he finally anchored in the Roman Church, he is seen as—not tolerant, for that would involve dogmatic points on which he was most jealous, but—sympathetic in all that was of interest to England, and ready to recognize what was good and high in the English Church.[2]

To say that Newman, while still an Anglican, changed from intolerance and outspoken criticism of the claims of the Roman Church to an attitude of tolerance and finally of intellectual acceptance, seems in clear harmony with the testimony of the *Apologia pro Vita Sua*, that psychological autobiography which is among the most self-revealing of English literature.[3]

[2] R. W. Church, *Occasional Papers* (London: Macmillan and Co., 1897), II, 470.

[3] Newman, with his keen introspection, had a decided consciousness of the various stages through which he passed. In the *Apologia* he reprints a letter which he wrote in 1849 in refutation of the charge that he had been, during the last ten years of his life in the Anglican Church, a "concealed Romanist." After explaining that the term, obviously meant to impute moral blame, must have been understood to designate "one, who, professing to belong to the Church of England, in his heart and will intends to benefit the Church of Rome, at the expense of the Church of England," he added: "In the sense in which

Dean Church was not guilty of exaggeration when he wrote that Newman, during his first productive years, was "intolerant, even to harshness, to the Roman Church." To John Henry Newman as a boy, the Catholic religion was known only by name.[4] If there were, even at that time, the tiny beginnings at work in his soul of the grace that would one day lead him into the Catholic Church, he became conscious of it only much later.[5] His first deep religious impressions, received at the age of fifteen, were, to use his own words, "Calvinistic in character." [6] He speaks of an "inward conversion" which he was aware of at that time, and which he was convinced "would last into the next life" as his election to eternal glory.[7] During this same period his reading of Newton on the Prophecies assured him that the pope was the Antichrist predicted by Daniel, St. Paul, and St. John, and he writes in the

---

I have explained the words, I can simply and honestly say that I was not a concealed Romanist during the whole, or any part of, the years in question. For the first four years of the ten, (up to Michaelmas, 1839,) I honestly wished to benefit the Church of England, at the expense of the Church of Rome: for the second four years I wished to benefit the Church of England without prejudice to the Church of Rome: at the beginning of the ninth year (Michaelmas, 1843) I began to despair of the Church of England, and gave up all clerical duty; and then, what I wrote and did was influenced by a mere wish not to injure it, and not by the wish to benefit it: at the beginning of the tenth year I distinctly contemplated leaving it, but I also distinctly told my friends that it was in my contemplation" (*Apo.*, pp. 186 f.).

[4] Cf. *ibid.*, p. 2.
[5] Cf. *ibid.*, pp. 2 f.
[6] Wilfrid Ward, *op. cit.*, I, 30; cf. also *Apo.*, p. 4.
[7] *Apo.*, p. 4.

Apologia: "My imagination was stained by the effects of this doctrine up to the year 1843; it had been obliterated from my reason and judgment at an earlier date; but the thought remained upon me as a sort of false conscience." [8]

The influence of Oxford University, where he entered in June, 1817, as a resident of Trinity, and where he became a fellow of Oriel in 1822, was not calculated to increase Newman's love for Catholicism. Hilaire Belloc, writing of the real heroism required in Newman's eventual conversion, thus describes his position at Oxford:

. . . Newman was not only of Oxford, nor only in Oxford; he was, if one may use the metaphor, Oxford itself. He trembled with delight in his membership of this essentially anti-Catholic body, and when I say "essentially anti-Catholic" I mean the very word I use—"essentially." . . . To have been an undergraduate at Oxford College was his happiest memory. To be elected a Fellow of an Oxford College his proudest moment. He lived within an extremely narrow Oxford circle, responding vividly to its every function. [9]

The years between Newman's election to Oriel and his resignation of his fellowship in 1845, a few days before he entered the Catholic Church, were crowded years indeed. They saw Newman develop from the bashful youth of 1821 to the brilliant leader of the

[8] *Ibid.,* p. 7.
[9] *Apologia pro Vita Sua,* edited for college use by Daniel M. O'Connell, S.J., with a Foreword by Hilaire Belloc (Chicago: Loyola University Press, 1930), p. x.

Tractarian movement, whose Sunday afternoon sermon at St. Mary's was the event of the Oxford week. They saw him gradually lose confidence in the scholarly *tour de force* by which he had constructed his persuasive paper theory of the *via media* to justify an Anglican position midway between the Protestantism of the Reformers and the Church of Rome. They saw him, finally, unsettled by the systematic study of the Fathers which he had begun in 1828, enter into the retirement of Littlemore, to emerge only as a member of the very Church he had once so vigorously opposed.[10]

During these years, strong influences were at work, which were to do much toward shaping the future form of Newman's theological thought. About 1823 he read Bishop Butler's *Analogy of Religion*, and was particularly impressed by two points, which were, as he writes in the *Apologia:*

First, the very idea of an analogy between the separate works of God leads to the conclusion that the system which is of less importance is economically or sacramentally connected with the more momentous system. . . . Secondly, Butler's doctrine that Probability is the guide of life, led me, at least under the teaching to which a few years later I was introduced, to the question of the logical cogency of Faith, on which I have written so much.[11]

[10] This period of his life has been fully described by Newman in the course of the *Apologia*, and has been summarized by Wilfrid Ward, *op. cit.*, Vol. I, chap. 2.

[11] *Apo.*, pp. 10 f. Newman calls these "the underlying principles of a great portion of my teaching." This is certainly true in the sense

The year 1827 witnessed the appearance of John Keble's *The Christian Year*. The two main intellectual contributions which it made to Newman's formation were developments of what he had learned from Butler. First was the "Sacramental system" which Newman calls ". . . a doctrine, which embraces, in its fulness, not only what Anglicans, as well as Catholics, believe about Sacraments properly so called; but also the article of 'the Communion of Saints;' and likewise the Mysteries of the faith." [12] The other was the fact that Keble ascribed the firmness of assent that we give to religious doctrine not to the probabilities which were its introduction, but to the power of the love and faith that prompted its acceptance.[13] It was to supplement what he perceived to be the limitations of this explanation that Newman introduced considerations of his own on the subject in his *University Sermons*, *Essay on Ecclesiastical Miracles*, the *Essay on the Development of Christian Doctrine*,[14] and finally in the *Grammar of Assent*.

To the influence of books there was added the in-

---

that they first inspired in him trains of thought which he later developed at considerable length in his writings. We shall treat later of the "underlying principles" of Newman's theological thought in another sense; that is, the principles of religion as Newman conceived it, and in the light of which his separate theological speculations must be viewed before we can be sure that we are interpreting them as he intended.

[12] *Ibid.*, p. 18.
[13] *Ibid.*, p. 19.
[14] Cf. *ibid.*, p. 20.

fluence of friends. Of Hurrell Froude, with whom he was intimate from 1829 until Froude's untimely death in 1836, Newman writes: "It is difficult to enumerate the precise additions to my theological creed which I derived from a friend to whom I owe so much. He taught me to look with admiration towards the Church of Rome, and in the same degree to dislike the Reformation. He fixed deep in me the idea of devotion to the Blessed Virgin, and he led me gradually to believe in the Real Presence." [15] The acquaintance with the ideas of Hurrell Froude was an important factor in Newman's eventual transition to that phase of his progress in which he became, according to Dean Church, intolerant to the English Church and tolerant to the Roman.[16]

Among the works which Newman wrote during his fellowship at Oriel are such masterly treatments as *The Arians of the Fourth Century*, the *Lectures on Justification*, *Select Treatises of St. Athanasius*, the *Essays on Miracles*, the *Parochial and Plain Sermons*, and the *Oxford University Sermons*. They are distinctly Anglican in tone, which is surely to be expected, but they bear also the unmistakable marks of the various stages of Newman's Romeward progress.

[15] *Ibid.*, p. 25.
[16] The reader will find an excellent summary of the various early influences on Newman's theology in the chapter entitled "The Sources of Newman's Psychology of Faith," in Sylvester P. Juergens, S.M., *Newman on the Psychology of Faith in the Individual* (New York: The Macmillan Company, 1928), pp. 235–60.

We have a particularly striking example of the evolution of Newman's theological thought in the two essays on miracles, republished in the same volume in
1870 and in the subsequent editions of Newman's
works. These essays are extremely difficult to reconcile if we divorce our study of them from a consideration of the different years in which they were
written.[17]

[17] The first essay, addressed chiefly to religious inquirers and treating the miracles of Scripture as of a nature evidential to the truth
of the revelation they accompanied, was composed in the years 1825–
26, while Newman was under the influence of Middleton's *On the
Miracles of the Early Church*. (Cf. *Apo.*, p. 14.) It is admirable for
its insistence on the importance of the final cause in determination of
the antecedent credibility of a miracle. (Cf. *Mir.*, pp. 18, 20, 26.) But
in his development of this point, Newman argues to the credibility
of the Scripture miracles from the contrast with others "unworthy
of an All-wise Author," such as "many of the Miracles related by
the Fathers," and the "Miracles of the Romish Breviary," from their
frequent strangeness and "want of decorum." (Cf. *Mir.*, pp. 28–31.)
This first essay abounds with disparaging comments on the miracles
of the "Papists," "who seem desirous of answering the unbeliever's
demand for a perpetual Miracle" (*Mir.*, p. 41). "The notorious insincerity and frauds of the Church of Rome in other things," he writes
on page 77, "are in themselves enough to throw a strong suspicion
on its testimony to its own miracles." (In the 1870 and later editions,
Newman's own notes repudiating these and other aspersions are an-
nexed to the text.)
The second essay was written in 1842–43, and, while still definitely
Anglican in tone, shows a marked change of attitude. Here Newman
is writing on the Ecclesiastical Miracles, as addressed to Christians
in reward of faith and as forming matter for devotion. In the introductory chapter he observes: "Ecclesiastical Miracles, that is, Miracles
posterior to the Apostolic age, are on the whole different in object,
character, and evidence, from those of Scripture on the whole, so
that one series or family ought never to be confounded with the
other; yet . . . the former are not therefore at once to be rejected"
(*Mir.*, pp. 99–100). Entire sections of this essay are devoted to whole
or partial refutations of the positions maintained in the first. (Cf.,
for example, sections 48–50 and 54.) Newman, who wrote the second

His gradual approach to Rome was for a long time an intellectual drift whose inevitable goal Newman, firm in his loyalty to the Church of his birth although impatient of her faults, failed to perceive. What determined Newman's advance was, after all, his mind inclining toward the truth, not his will consciously seeking adherence to the Roman Catholic Church.

With his conversion in 1845, his quest for the true Church, the Church of the Fathers he revered, reached its logical conclusion. Of the state of his mind since the day of his reception into the Church, he wrote in 1864:

From the time that I became a Catholic, of course I have no further history of my religious opinions to narrate. In saying this, I do not mean to say that my mind has been idle, or that I have given up thinking on theological subjects; but that I have had no variations to record, and have had no anxiety of heart whatever. I have been in perfect peace and contentment; I never have had one doubt. I was not conscious to myself, on my conversion, of any change, intellectual or moral, wrought in my mind. I was not conscious of firmer faith in the fundamental truths of Revelation, or of more self-command; I had not more fervour; but it was like coming

---

essay during the period in which he "wished to benefit the Church of England without prejudice to the Church of Rome," has abandoned entirely his use of the Catholic Church as a horrible example.

When the two essays were republished together in 1879, Newman prefaced them with an explanation in which he admitted that in the Essay on Scripture Miracles he had gone beyond both the needs and claims of his argument when, in order to show the special dignity and beauty of such miracles, he had depreciated the purpose and value of the miracles of Church history. (Cf. *Mir.*, p. viii.)

into port after a rough sea; and my happiness on that score remains to this day without interruption.[18]

From November, 1846, until his ordination to the Catholic priesthood on May 30, 1847, the new convert studied at the *Collegio di Propaganda* in Rome. His acquaintance with Catholic theology as taught in the seminary was therefore a short one; and even at best, if we may credit the information which he relays in one of his letters to J. D. Dalgairns, the theology taught in Rome during that period, some years before the Thomistic revival sponsored by Leo XIII, was not very systematic.[19] It is at any rate certain that Newman's brief stay in Rome produced no appreciable difference in the form of his theological argument. In his own writings he did not adopt the conventional scholastic phraseology. The fact of conversion does

[18] *Apo.*, p. 238.
[19] "Hope told me we should find very little theology here, and a talk we had yesterday with one of the Jesuit fathers here shows we shall find little philosophy. It arose from our talking of the Greek studies of the Propaganda, and asking whether the youths learned Aristotle. 'Oh no,' he said, 'Aristotle is in no favour here—no, not in Rome—nor St. Thomas. I have read Aristotle and St. Thomas and owe a great deal to them, but they are out of favour here and throughout Italy. St. Thomas is a great saint—people don't care to speak against him; they profess to reverence him, but put him aside.' I asked what philosophy they did adopt. He said *none*. 'Odds and ends—whatever seems to them best—like St. Clement's Stromata. They have no philosophy. *Facts* are the great things, and nothing else. Exegesis, but not doctrine.' He went on to say that many privately were sorry for this, many Jesuits, he said; but no one dared to oppose the fashion" (Wilfrid Ward, *op. cit.*, I, 166 f.). The "Hope" referred to is James R. Hope-Scott, later a convert himself.

not deprive a man of his intellectual background, nor does it give him a new one. Newman did not become overnight a theologian of the Schools.

From the time of his return to England several months after ordination to establish there the Oratory of St. Philip Neri, Newman's life was one of continual labor and frequent disappointment. To this latter period of his life belong some of his finest writings, including the *Difficulties of Anglicans*, the *Discourses to Mixed Congregations*, *The Idea of a University*, *The Present Position of Catholics in England*, the *Sermons on Various Occasions*, and the *Essay in Aid of a Grammar of Assent*.

Newman's Catholic years, however, were shadowed by disagreements with the policies of Monsignor (afterward Archbishop and Cardinal) Manning, and with the school of thought represented by the editor of the powerful *Dublin Review*, William George Ward. Monsignor George Talbot, chamberlain to Pope Pius IX, seems often to have represented Newman's ideas and interests to the Vatican authorities in the worst possible light. The suit for libel entered against Newman by the apostate priest, Dr. Giacinto Achilli, was the source of tremendous anxiety for many months. Attempts to lay the lasting foundations for a Catholic university in Ireland were in vain.

For several years before the publication of the *Apologia pro Vita Sua* in 1863, Newman had been in virtual retirement, almost forgotten by the public and ignored by the English press. As Wilfrid Ward remarks, had Cardinal Newman died just after his sixty-third birthday his career would have been catalogued as the saddest of failures.[20]

The triumphant success of the *Apologia* marked the turning of the tide. From then until the official coronation of his labors in his elevation to the cardinalate by Leo XIII in 1879, John Henry Newman, while still not free from opposition in influential circles, was a power in England, and his utterances were received with universal respect. The last eleven years of his life, as a cardinal of the Catholic Church, were years of peace and joy, and of grateful recognition by Catholic and Protestant alike. His death brought forth expressions of deepest sorrow from every corner of England. The eulogy preached in the London Oratory church by Cardinal Manning began with the words: "We have lost our greatest witness for the faith. . . ."

[20] Cf. *op. cit.*, I, 10.

CHAPTER II

NEWMAN'S PLACE AMONG CATHOLIC THEOLOGIANS

As a theologian, John Henry Newman is hard to catalogue. He was certainly not of the Thomistic school; his works betray little or no dependence on the study of the Angelic Doctor.[1] Nor was he a Scholastic in the sense of following either of the other two schools, Molinist or Scotist, into which the great majority of non-Thomistic theologians may be grouped today. But although Newman had, as we have seen, almost no training in the theology of the Schools, we must not for that reason automatically picture him as an opponent of the principles which underlie Scholastic theology. Arnold Lunn, we think, was guilty of an oversimplification when he wrote, before his con-

[1] But it is not correct to assert, as does Thomas J. Gerrard in the article "Bergson, Newman and Aquinas" in *The Catholic World* for March, 1913 (Vol. XCVI, p. 756), that "From the beginning to the end of Newman's works there is no mention of St. Thomas." There are eloquent tributes to the Angelic Doctor and his theology in the *Historical Sketches*, II, 226 f., and in the *Idea*, pp. 469 f. St. Thomas is quoted in the *Letter to the Duke of Norfolk* (*Diff.*, II, 256), and in the *Grammar of Assent*, p. 503. Newman refers to his sanctity and influence in the *Discourses to Mixed Congregations*, p. 99, and in the *Present Position of Catholics in England*, p. 396.

16

version to Catholicism: "No contrast could be greater than the contrast between the official Roman Catholicism of the Schools, and the philosophy which led Newman from a belief in God to a belief in the Pope. Scholastic theology is based on reason, whereas with Newman, Faith always came before Reason." [2]

The truth of the matter is that, according to Newman as well as the Scholastics, theology is founded on faith in the revealed truths, from which conclusions are drawn by the use of reason. Treating of the action of logic as applied to the scientific analysis of revealed truth, Newman has this to say:

Reason, thus considered, is subservient to faith, as handling, examining, explaining, recording, cataloguing, defending, the truths which faith, not reason, has gained for us, as providing an intellectual expression of supernatural facts, eliciting what is implicit, comparing, measuring, connecting each with each, and forming one and all into a theological system. [3]

While not intended as a systematic definition of theology, this statement of the case, in its view of the relative roles of faith and reason, is in complete agreement with the traditional definitions of the Schools. [4]

[2] *Roman Converts* (London: Chapman and Hall, 1924), p. 63.
[3] *Dev.*, p. 336.
[4] In *The Concept of Sacred Theology* (Milwaukee: Bruce, 1941), p. 2, Rev. Dr. Joseph Clifford Fenton, discussing the common modern definitions of sacred theology (he refers to more than twenty such definitions), writes: "All of these common definitions of sacred theology agree in describing it in function of its source. In this description they are perfectly accurate. The theologian actually draws conclusions from principles which are true and are accepted as such

Undoubtedly Newman has written most eloquently of the importance of faith. It is also true that in his opposition to the spirit of Liberalism in religion, which glorified man's reasoning powers to a dangerous excess, Newman sometimes treated human reason in a rather disparaging fashion. But it is a mistake to believe that he was under any illusion about the relationship of faith and reason in religion and theology.

In spite of this basic and essential agreement with the scholastic theologians, it still does not seem that we can class Newman as a Scholastic himself. He was not sufficiently familiar with, nor did he make extensive enough use of, the traditional resources of scientific procedure developed by the centuries of exposition, discussion, and controversy among the great theologians of the Church. Likewise in the matter of terminology his divergence from traditional theology is

---

with the highest degree of certitude. He proceeds in a rigorously scientific manner, and thus he develops a human discipline and utilizes the force of human reason. At the same time the principles out of which the theologian draws his conclusions are actually truths which have been revealed to the world by God through Jesus Christ our Lord. He would have no reason for accepting his conclusions as true if he did not assent to the principles from which they are drawn with the acceptance of divine faith. In so far, then, as sacred theology draws out the implications and inferences contained in divine teaching, it is truly the 'science of faith.' " Dr. Fenton goes on to develop a more adequate notion of theology than that contained in the usual theological texts. We do not set down the passage quoted above as Dr. Fenton's definition of theology, but merely to show the agreement as to the parts played by faith and reason in the writings of Newman and of the modern Scholastics.

marked by the absence from his works of the scientific phraseology and *axiomata* which have been accepted in the Schools.[5]

Newman was not a systematic theologian. He never erected, nor did he intend to erect, an articulated theological structure. One of the great injustices that have been done to Newman is the synthetic development, from a Newman principle, of a sort of system by his "disciples." The Modernists, for instance, attempted to stretch parts of the *Essay on Development* into a system which attacked the objective value of the dogmas of the Church. Not only was such a "system" never intended by Newman; it was also one that he would have detested, and that ran directly counter to the principles which, as we shall see, Newman himself asserted to be at the base of his religious thought.

Although Newman was not a systematic theologian, we might say, broadly speaking, that all his works are theological, in the sense that his theological reflections and opinions pervade and color all his writings. The classification of Newman's works by the publishers of the uniform edition into eight categories—Sermons,

[5] Describing "Newman's disdain for the trammels of technical phraseology," Wilfrid Ward notes: "This was partly a matter of principle. Newman held that the thinkers were constantly the victims of phraseology both in philosophy and theology, and that technical language, so valuable in the interests of clearness, was ever being perverted. It could not, like algebraic symbols, be left to work automatically, but must be constantly tested by comparison with actual thought" (*op. cit.*, II, 505).

Treatises, Historical, Essays, Theological, Polemical, Literary, and Devotional [6]—is largely a matter of form, not of contents. There is, for example, a brilliant exposition of the confusion of the Anglican ideas about the unity of the Visible Church in a work which is professedly a novel: [7] and Newman's ideas on the relationship of theology and the physical sciences are found in a volume on university education.[8]

It is almost universally admitted that Newman's major contributions to theology have been in the literature on faith. Under this head we may group Newman's theories on the development of Christian doctrine, set forth tentatively in the *Oxford University Sermons* and definitively in the *Essay on Development*, as Newman's treatment of *what* we believe; and his teachings on the nature of belief, which reached their full maturity in the *Grammar of Assent*, as his answer to the question *why* the average man believes.

Largely because of these two theories, Newman has sometimes been called the father of the "new apologetics." The term "new apologetics" has fallen into

[6] This is the classification which is published in the advertisements in several of the volumes of the uniform edition, and in volume one of the Wilfrid Ward *Life of John Henry Cardinal Newman*. It has been adopted by the editor of the Loyola University Press edition of the *Apologia*.

[7] Cf. *Loss and Gain*, pp. 301–5. The same work contains one of the most widely quoted of all Newman passages, that on the Mass, pp. 327–29. As a study in the psychology of conversion, *Loss and Gain* is second only to the *Apologia*.

[8] Cf. *Idea*, Discourses 3, 4, and 9. Also pp. 428–79.

disrepute among the better modern theologians; and deservedly so, when the label is applied to an apologetical method which exaggerates the importance of the internal, immanent motives of assent to the credibility of revelation, at the expense of the traditional exterior proofs based on miracles and prophecies. The argument from conscience always had a strong appeal to Newman personally as a proof for the existence of God; but no one who has read the *Essays on Miracles* could accuse Newman of underestimating the value or of misunderstanding the function of these sensible supernatural phenomena as criteria of a true divine revelation.

Newman's major theological contributions are not a substitute for traditional apologetics. They are auxiliary to it. We might say that they are a preliminary to apologetics, in the sense that they are directed against a modern mentality which is the fruit of an ingrained prejudice and a certain intellectual slovenliness, and which too often prevents the scientific Catholic apologetics from accomplishing its end.

The modern mind is slow to admit the credibility of Christian revelation partly because it possesses no real idea of what valid grounds of credibility are. In the *Grammar of Assent,* Newman has given a psychological analysis of the grounds for belief in the average individual. He emphasizes the point that a man may believe in Christian revelation on grounds of credibility at least as strong—we are here considering only the natural light of human reason—as those of cherished beliefs which not even the most "modern" of men would think of questioning. Once this point is established, the foundation stone has been laid for the appreciation of the probative force of the traditional apologetics of the Church.

As a sad heritage of almost two centuries of rationalist Liberalism, there is another prejudice, which engenders in the modern mind a disinclination to consider seriously the arguments of Catholic apologetics. The average "modern" does not bother to disagree with a particular dogma of the Church. He simply dismisses the whole idea of dogma. Newman, in the *Essay on Development*, shows the inevitability of the growth of dogma in Christianity. Anyone who reads the *Essay* with a fairly open mind, while he may differ from Newman on details, will find it difficult to maintain any longer in his mind the chimera of a non-dogmatic Christianity, and his prejudice against listening to the arguments of Catholic apologetics will have been seriously weakened.

When we speak (as we shall henceforth without reservation) of Newman as a theologian, or of his theology, it must be clearly understood that we do not imply that he was a professedly scientific theologian in the usual meaning of the term. He constructed no system. He belonged to no theological school.

Newman must not be considered and judged as a scholastic theologian, which he was not and did not pretend to be. He was a keen thinker and illuminating writer on certain theological problems, with an intuitive appreciation of the difficulties of the modern mind. This appreciation resulted in an original and effective approach to the religious questions and controversies of his time. The rare delicacy with which his mind was attuned to the needs of his age has assured the permanent interest and value of work that was primarily polemic and occasional.

Newman's major works constitute a highly useful modern approach to the traditional apologetics of the Church. He has made a real and significant contribution to English theological literature. We may agree or disagree with many of his conclusions. It would be short-sighted indeed to dismiss his theological thought as inconsequential because it lies for the most part along the margin rather than in the central current of the theological stream.

CHAPTER III

THE FOUNDATIONS OF NEWMAN'S
RELIGIOUS THOUGHT

IT DOES not seem that we are taking too much for granted when we assume that any reader of Newman should wish to determine, not merely what a certain argument might be construed as meaning if torn from the ensemble of Newman's works, but what it was intended to mean by Newman himself. Now, if there are certain fundamental principles on which Newman's whole idea of religion is based, the presumption must be that Newman, in a particular section of his works, did not intend to sabotage his entire conception of religion by contradicting these principles.

In the *Apologia pro Vita Sua*, Newman wrote:

From the age of fifteen, dogma has been the fundamental principle of my religion: I know no other religion; I cannot enter into the idea of any other sort of religion; religion, as a mere sentiment, is to me a dream and a mockery. As well can there be filial love without the fact of a father, as devotion without the fact of a Supreme Being. What I held in 1816, I held in 1833, and I hold in 1864. Please God, I shall hold it to the end. . . .

Secondly, I was confident in the truth of a certain definite religious teaching, based upon this foundation of dogma;

viz. that there was a visible Church, with sacraments and rites which are the channels of invisible grace. I thought that this was the doctrine of Scripture, of the early Church, and of the Anglican Church. Here again, I have not changed in opinion; I am as certain now on this point as I was in 1833, and have never ceased to be certain.[1]

This passage from the *Apologia* is of prime importance for the true interpretation of Newman. It records, on the authority of the Cardinal himself, two basic doctrines which he never repudiated. For the student desirous of knowing the exact meaning which Newman intended in a particular passage, these two principles are invaluable; they act as the twin lenses of the stereoscope through which an isolated segment of Newman's thought may be seen in perspective with its background.

Some time after we had written the preceding paragraphs, we came across a confirmation of our theory in *Religion and Reality*, by J. H. Tuckwell.[2] The author of this work is interested in finding the "one identical experience" by reason of which we class Christianity, Mohammedanism, Zoroastrianism, and Buddhism "under one common name and call them all 'religion.' "[3] If we find such a common denom-

---

[1] *Apo.*, p. 49. On pages 52 f., Newman mentions a third belief which he held in 1833, that "the Church of Rome was bound up with the cause of Antichrist by the Council of Trent." But this idea, he writes, he has "utterly renounced and trampled upon since."

[2] James Henry Tuckwell, *Religion and Reality, a Study in the Philosophy of Mysticism* (London: Methuen and Co., 1915).

[3] *Ibid.*, p. 2.

inator, it seems to him, we shall find "the essence of religion." [4] He is regretfully forced to admit, however, that in such a search, Cardinal Newman is absolutely useless as a guide. His reason is intriguing:

Into what fatal error and confusion the noblest and subtlest minds fall when religion is identified with creed or ritual is notorious, and was never more conspicuously illustrated than, for example, in the case of Cardinal Newman. . . . As to the lustre of his genius there is no question, and there is no need to do more than refer to it here. Yet with all his incomparable gifts of intellect and heart, as a religious guide impartial judgment is obliged reluctantly to pronounce him an almost total failure. . . . The reason is to be found chiefly in the invincible dogmatic bias of his mind, in a constitutional incapacity to distinguish the essence of religion from its form, its substance from its shadow. From this source spring what often surprises us in so great and gracious a mind, an amazing childish credulity, and, it must be confessed, at times a faltering sense of truth. In his "Apologia pro Vita Sua," he frankly acknowledges his dogmatic prejudice. "From the age of fifteen," he writes, "dogma has been the fundamental principle of my religion; I cannot enter into the idea of any other sort of religion. Religion as a mere sentiment is to me a dream and a mockery." . . . Now on such a theory as Newman's there can be consistently only two classes of religion—The True and The False—the true religion, of course, being held alone by those who believe the correct dogmas.[5]

The author, who is interested in reducing religion to an experience based on man's feeling of need for

[4] *Ibid.*, p. 3.
[5] *Ibid.*, pp. 4, 5, 6.

something higher than himself to worship,[6] thus rejects Newman because for Newman the fundamental principle of religion was *dogma*.

Of course we have no sympathy for the thesis advanced in the volume under discussion. And we have, incidentally, searched it in vain for any justification of the gratuitous assertion that the great Cardinal had "at times, a faltering sense of truth." But we admire the author both for his discernment and for his frank admission of the fact that the name of Newman can never be linked with an idea of religion which disregards dogmatic truth in favor of "feeling" or sentiment. This is a compliment to the Cardinal, and one all the more striking because it is so unintentional.

It is Newman's lifelong adherence to the dogmatic principle that explains his constant hostility to the spirit of Liberalism in religion, which strove to "free" humanity from the trammels of religious authority, and which Newman recognized for what it was, "the anti-dogmatic principle and its developments."[7] The

[6] "We have seen that everywhere religion arises from man's feeling of need, of weakness, of incompleteness, of limitation, and a consequent impulse to surmount it by union of some kind with beings possessed of powers of life higher than his own, of whom in one way or another he has succeeded in framing to himself some conception. This worship of powers higher than himself from a sense of need is thus the essential feature of religion" (*ibid.*, pp. 38 f.).

[7] *Apo.*, p. 48. In a note which did not appear in the first edition of the *Apologia*, Newman explains further what he means by "Liberalism": "Now by Liberalism I mean false liberty of thought, or the exercise of thought upon matters, in which, from the constitution of the human mind, thought cannot be brought to any successful issue, and therefore is out of place. Among such matters are first principles

struggle against Liberalism furnished the bond of unity, as it provided the motive force, of Newman's writings. All his works, in varying degrees and different manners, from his publications as an Anglican down through the final productions of his life, were intended to play their part in the conflict, directly or indirectly. "The nineteenth century," writes Douglas Woodruff, "was the supreme century of liberalism, and Newman was the greatest enemy modern liberalism has ever had to meet. He was the enemy of liberalism because liberalism was the enemy of revelation." [8]

of whatever kind; and of these the most sacred and momentous are especially to be reckoned the truths of Revelation. Liberalism then is the mistake of subjecting to human judgment those revealed doctrines which are in their nature beyond and independent of it, and of claiming to determine on intrinsic grounds the truth and value of propositions which rest for their reception simply on the external authority of the Divine Word" (*Apo.*, p. 288).

[8] *For Hilaire Belloc, Essays in Honor of His 71st Birthday*, edited by Douglas Woodruff (New York: Sheed and Ward, 1942), p. 32. Cf. also *Apo.*, pp. 34 f. Wilfrid Ward writes: ". . . after the brilliant apprenticeship at Oxford and the few years in which the 'Oxford Plato,' the friend of Blanco White and of Whately, showed some tendency towards intellectualism, we see him from 1828 onwards undergoing a profound religious reaction, which grew into the conviction that he had a definite mission in life. And what was that mission? It was one of relentless war against the 'Liberalism' in thought that was breaking up ancient institutions in Church and State, and would not cease from its work until it had destroyed religion. In England its aims were comparatively moderate and its tendencies disguised, but we are now witnessing its inevitable results in Continental Europe. Newman foresaw them in 1828. He saw fresh symptoms of an un-Christian movement in the revolution of 1830 in France, and on one occasion refused even to look at the tricolor that was hoisted on the mast of a French ship" (*op. cit.*, I, 4 f.). A. E. Baker remarks of Newman: "His opposition to liberalism . . . was the

Later on in this study we shall have occasion to consider in some detail a fact which is one of the ironies of
history: that enemies of Catholic dogma should have
attempted to hide in the shadow of a man whose guiding motive in life was the defense of the dogmatic
principle.

---

most consistent motive of his life" (*Prophets for an Age of Doubt.*
London: The Centenary Press, 1934), p. 140. Cf. also Sylvester P.
Juergens, *op. cit.*, pp. 2 f.; and J. D. Folghera, *op. cit.*, pp. 17 f.

CHAPTER IV

NEWMAN'S THEOLOGICAL METHOD

WHILE the fundamental tenets of Newman's religious thought, and the motive guiding its expression, must never be ignored by the reader if Newman's works are to be viewed in true proportion, there are other aspects of Newman's theology which must be taken into account also. One of the elements essential to an understanding of Newman is an appreciation of the method he employed in the expression of his theological thought.

Newman was primarily a controversialist. He was of a practical turn of mind which discouraged abstract theorizing. Whenever possible, he preferred to base his arguments on the history of the early Church and on the writings of the Fathers. These three constituents might almost be said to form the substance of Newman's theological method.

First, Newman's special field was that of controversy. His expositions of Catholic doctrine were usually made in refutation of a particular objection, attack, or error. In a letter written from the Birmingham Oratory and dated February 18, 1866, he wrote to W. G. Ward: "As to writing a volume on the Pope's infallibility, it never so much as entered into my thought. I am a controversialist, not a theologian, and I should have nothing to say about it."[1]

Although he thus refused to write, ex professo, a theological treatise on infallibility, he did issue an effective defense of the doctrine when the controversial occasion arose with the publication of Gladstone's pamphlet attacking the decrees of the Vatican Council.[2]

As a controversialist, Newman was no mere facile debater, eager to make telling minor points even at the expense of antagonizing his opponent. In the eyes of a less conscientious polemicist, Newman would appear almost painfully fair. Not only does he set forth the case for the opposition as clearly as he can, but the keenness of his insight into the minds of his adversaries sometimes results in a more reasonable statement of their position than they have been able to construct themselves.

It was Newman's controversial practice to clear the ground for the establishment of the point at issue by conceding, for the sake of argument, as much as pos-

[1] Edmund Sheridan Purcell, Life of Cardinal Manning (London: Macmillan and Co., 1896), II, 322.

[2] The Vatican Decrees in Their Bearing on Civil Allegiance, by the Right Hon. W. E. Gladstone, M.P. (published in the United States by D. Appleton and Company, New York, 1874). Newman's reply, which took the form of a Letter to the Duke of Norfolk, is included in the Difficulties of Anglicans, II, 171 f.

sible to the position of his opponents. Speaking of Tract 71, which he wrote several years before his conversion, Newman attributes its gentle spirit toward the Church of Rome to the fact that ". . . the Tract, being controversial, assumes as little and grants as much as possible on the points in dispute, and insists on points of agreement as well as of difference." [3] Although the passing years saw Newman abandon his first position in the controversy between Anglicanism and Catholicism and pass over to the Catholic side, his controversial method remained the same.

A second aspect of Newman's theological method is his avoidance of elaborate speculation and dialectic. This was owing both to the constitution of his own mind and, as we shall see, to his knowledge of the intellectual character of his English audience. Even in the *Grammar of Assent*, which is probably the most complicated of his works, his purpose is to prove, not the value of "paper logic," but the importance of realizing, in any analysis of the nature of belief, the function of the living intellect following its own internal laws. The quotation from St. Ambrose which Newman prefaces to the *Grammar* might well be taken as his own watchword in theological writing: "Non in dialecticâ complacuit Deo salvum facere populum suum." [4]

---

[3] *Apo.*, p. 64.
[4] *G.A.*, title page.

The third characteristic of Newman's theological method is his preference for positive argument based on the interpretation of the facts of early Church history and on the writings of the Fathers. He was a profound student of both fields, and his ability to make the primitive ages of the Church live again in his works is the result of the vividness of color and outline with which these centuries lived in his own mind.

There is no contradiction in the fact that Newman was at once an original thinker and a disciple of the Fathers. We might even say that one of the elements of Newman's originality was his dependence on antiquity. He began his theological writing in the Church of England, which distrusted antiquity's testimony; and he lived in an age when the blossoming "scientific" mentality despised it. In a period when it is the intellectual fashion to deride the wisdom of the past, the true antiquarian may be the most original of men.

There are a few sentences in Newman's famous *Letter to Dr. Pusey* which deserve quoting for the light they throw upon his predilections in theological discussion:

> For myself, hopeless as you consider it, I am not ashamed still to take my stand upon the Fathers, and do not mean to budge. The history of their times is not yet an old almanac to me. Of course I maintain the value and authority of the "Schola" as one of the *loci theologici;* nevertheless I sympathize with Petavius in preferring to the "contentious and subtle theology" of the middle age, that "more elegant and

fruitful teaching which is moulded after the image of erudite antiquity." The Fathers made me a Catholic, and I am not going to kick down the ladder by which I ascended into the Church. It is a ladder quite as serviceable for that purpose now, as it was twenty years ago. Though I hold, as you know, a process of development in Apostolic truth as time goes on, such development does not supersede the Fathers, but explains and completes them. And, in particular, as regards our teaching concerning the Blessed Virgin, with the Fathers I am content. . . . Here, let me say, as on other points, the Fathers are enough for me. I do not wish to say more than they suggest to me, and will not say less.[5]

The *Letter to Dr. Pusey*, which contains this express profession of Newman's dependence on the Fathers of the Church, is in itself a characteristic example of Newman's use of the patristic argument. A major portion of the letter is devoted to an examination of the sentiments of the Fathers concerning the prerogatives of the Virgin Mother of God. Newman defends the doctrine of the Immaculate Conception, which Pusey had criticized in his *Eirenicon*,[6] by show-

[5] *Diff.*, II, pp. 24 f.
[6] E. B. Pusey, *An Eirenicon, In a Letter to the Author of "The Christian Year"* (New York: D. Appleton and Company, 1866). Treating of the prospects of a corporate union of the Anglican and Roman Catholic Churches, Pusey, in two lengthy sections of the volume, assailed what he considered the extravagances of Catholic doctrine and practice regarding, among other points, the devotion to the Blessed Virgin. He deplored the definition of the dogma of the Immaculate Conception: "Even amid our own recent troubles, we heard of the decision in 1854 in silent sorrow" (p. 118). Newman, in his reply, gently but clearly expressed his regret at Pusey's antagonistic tone. "There was one of old time," he wrote, "who wreathed his sword in myrtle; excuse me—you discharge your olive-branch as if from a catapult" (*Diff.*, II, 7).

ing that it is an immediate inference from the primitive doctrine that Mary is the second Eve.[7] To quote isolated passages from the eloquent, closely linked chain of testimony, would be to do it an injustice. It must be read in full to be appreciated.

In concentrating on the somewhat technical aspects of his theological method, we hope that we have not conveyed the impression that Newman's writings are in any way difficult or uninteresting to the lay reader. Through all his works there runs like a shining thread the golden Newman rhetoric. The richness of color and the variety of his prose, his instinct for the exact word or phrase to convey his thought, his gift of vivid illustration—all conspire to make his writings a delight even to those who in no manner share his opinions. He had, in addition, a subtle and delicate sense of humor. Although he was ordinarily far more concerned with the conversion of his opponents than with their demo-

[7] *Diff.*, II, 31–76. Another instance of Newman's skillful use of positive theological argument is his refutation of the Protestant Bishop Douglas, contained in the *Essay on Ecclesiastical Miracles*. Douglas, in his defense of the New Testament miracles against Hume, proposed "a criterion by which the true miracles recorded in the New Testament are distinguished from the spurious miracles of the Pagans and Papists." Newman, not directly defending the "Papists," but criticizing the Douglas "criterion," pointed out, with several examples, drawn in striking detail, of the miracles of the apostles, how the norm of judgment set up by Douglas would eliminate from consideration these miracles as well as those of the "Papists" (*Mir.*, pp. 201–6). Still another example of Newman's historical method of argument may be found in the last seven chapters of the *Essay on Development*, which are devoted to a series of demonstrations, from the action and writings of the early Church, of the genuine antiquity as to doctrinal truth of the dogmas of the Church of modern times.

lition, he could use irony and even ridicule when the occasion demanded; and anyone who has read the *Lectures on the Present Position of Catholics in England* can testify that he used them with devastating effect.[8]

Over and above the consummate artistry of Newman's style, there is about his works an aura of true and deep spirituality. His theological expositions were not written after the dissection-table manner of the usual theological textbook. When he treats of a subject dear to Catholic hearts, his words glow with genuine emotional fire. His thought has an intangible beauty which is not something superadded by a trick of expression, but which could come only from within. The lines, for example, in praise of the Mother of God contained in the *Letter to Pusey* are among the loveliest ever written in her honor. If it is true that "style is the man," the reader of Newman needs no evidence other than that of his writings to be certain that here was a man not only an intellectual and literary genius, but a humble, loving servant of his God.

[8] The first lecture, on the "Protestant View of the Catholic Church," is particularly interesting in this regard. In the last lecture occurs the brilliant summary: "Such, then, is Popular Protestantism, considered in its opposition to Catholics. Its truth is Establishment by law; its philosophy is Theory; its faith is Prejudice; its facts are Fictions; its reasonings Fallacies; and its security is Ignorance about those whom it is opposing. The Law says that white is black; Ignorance says, why not? Theory says it ought to be, Fallacy says it must be, Fiction says it is, and Prejudice says it shall be" (p. 371).

CHAPTER V

NEWMAN'S TEMPERAMENT

ON FEBRUARY 20, 1866, Monsignor George Talbot, Newman's untiring critic at the Papal Court, wrote to Henry Edward Manning, Archbishop of Westminster: "I have read Newman's letter to Pusey. The patristic argument is admirable and unanswerable, but there is nothing new in it. The introduction and some other passages are detestable. . . . Dr. Newman is more English than the English. His spirit must be crushed." [1]

The parts of the *Letter* which Monsignor Talbot found "detestable" were those in which Newman took occasion to criticize what he considered the extremist school among English Catholics. The members of this group were guilty, Newman believed, of proposing exaggerated interpretations of Catholic doctrine and of attempting to propagate in England certain Continental forms of devotion which were repellent to educated Englishmen of the nineteenth century.

[1] Purcell, *op. cit.*, II, 322 f.

If we are to understand, not only some of Newman's theological positions, but also the perpetual
criticism and not infrequent suspicion of which he
was the object during his lifetime, there are two aspects of the Newman temperament, or character if
you prefer, which we must not neglect to take into
account. Newman was a man of absolute intellectual
honesty. He was also an Englishman to the last fiber
of his being.

The *Letter to Dr. Pusey* may serve as well as any
of Newman's works as an example of what we mean.
The opposition it aroused in some quarters is almost a
type, though milder than most, of similar storms that
marked his life.[2]

Dr. Pusey, in his attack on Catholic teachings, had
quoted largely from the published views of Father
Faber and W. G. Ward. Newman commented:

These two authors are worthy of all consideration, at once
from their character and from their ability. . . . It is pleas-
ant to praise them for their real excellences; but why do you
rest on them as authorities? . . . I cannot, then, without re-
monstrance, allow you to identify the doctrine of our Oxford friends in question, on the two subjects I have mentioned,
with the present spirit or the prospective creed of Catholics;
or to assume, as you do, that, because they are thorough-

[2] For an account of the circumstances surrounding the *Letter to
Pusey* and its reception, cf. Dom Cuthbert Butler, *The Life and
Times of Bishop Ullathorne* (London: Burns, Oates, and Wash-
bourne, 1926), I, 354-68; also Wilfrid Ward, *op. cit.*, II, 99-118; and
Paul Thureau-Dangin, *La renaissance catholique en Angleterre au
XIX siècle*, Part III, 2d ed. (Paris: Librairie Plon, 1906), pp. 47-80.

going and relentless in their statements, therefore they are
the harbingers of a new age, when to show a deference to
Antiquity will be thought little else than a mistake.[8]

These lines, written though they are with all of Newman's gentleness and tact, are none the less a definite
repudiation of a school of thought which had always
the tacit and often the express approval of the Archbishop of Westminster.

To say that Newman's intellectual honesty kept him
in continual opposition to the party represented principally by Cardinal Manning and W. G. Ward is not
to imply a lack of honesty in the latter. They believed
that the interests of the Church were best served by
an authoritarian, uncompromising, aggressively Ultra-
montane policy. Newman could not adopt a policy in
the wisdom of which he did not in conscience concur.

Newman was keenly alive to the dangers of the
age in which he lived. He saw, far more clearly than
most men of his time, the peril, from an intellectual
standpoint, created by the spirit of Liberalism. The
difficulties proposed by Liberalism against faith and
religion in general were surrounded by a specious
atmosphere of "science," which ensured their popu-
larity.

Newman was convinced that these difficulties could
be met only by an enlightened and understanding
apologetic which would find new answers to new

[8] *Diff.*, II, 22–24.

questions.[4] To Manning and Ward, any attempt to meet the new difficulties on their own ground, to admit that they had an element of seriousness, or to manifest a sympathetic understanding of the state of mind of their proponents was a confession of weakness or even an attitude deserving of suspicion.

This policy of the Archbishop of Westminster and of the editor of the *Dublin Review* is not a difficult one to understand. The spirit of Liberalism was at war with revealed religion; which meant, as always, that it was mainly at war with the Catholic Church. In time of war there is an inevitable curtailment of free speech, and any appearance, however slight, of fraternizing with the enemy is decidedly suspect.

Newman, however, did not believe in rigid supression of speculation. His life was dedicated to the combat against the spirit of Liberalism in religion, but he had only respect and sympathy for the sincere and earnest student in any field of scientific research. As regards theology, Newman cherished the idea of free investigation, which he proposes, in the *Apologia*, as

[4] In an essay which Newman wrote for the *Atlantis* of January, 1859, and which is reprinted in *Historical Sketches*, II, 433 f., under the title "The Benedictine Schools," we find the following comment: "As the new Christian society, which Charlemagne inaugurated, grew, its intellect grew with it, and at last began to ask questions and propose difficulties, which *catenae* and commentaries could not solve. Hard-headed objectors were not to be subdued by the reverence for antiquity and the amenities of polite literature" (p. 478). There is little doubt that Newman regarded his own age as just such a time. Cf. Wilfrid Ward, *op. cit.*, I, 433 f.

characteristic of the Middle Ages. He felt that individual theologians, confident that the infallibility of the Vicar of Christ would keep them from ultimate error, should not be silenced before their theories were adequately discussed.[5]

For a man of Newman's temperament, the nineteenth century was a difficult period. The rising tide of Italian nationalism, sharing to the full the antireligious tendency of the political Liberalism of the times, first threatened and then usurped the temporal power of the papacy. Any disposition to discuss or to appear to limit the prerogatives of the Holy See was, in such circumstances, certain to provoke the dislike and suspicion of a large body of devoted Catholics who were outspoken and fiercely loyal defenders of the pope. Still, Newman did not hide his distaste for the confident dogmatism with which W. G. Ward, in the pages of the *Dublin*, propagated his extremely broad interpretations of the scope and extent of papal infallibility and for the manner in which Ward stigmatized as unsound all Catholics who disagreed with him.[6] It was not that Newman lacked either loyalty or obedience to the Holy See; surely his whole life bears witness to that. But he was congenitally incapable

[5] Cf. *Apo.*, pp. 266 f.
[6] W. G. Ward was a capable lay theologian, but not greatly restrained in his language. Readers interested in his method of argument may consult *The Dublin Review*, January, 1865, article "The Encyclical and Syllabus," pp. 441-99; and April, 1865, article "Extent of the Church's Infallibility—The Encyclical 'Mirari Vos,'" pp. 41-69.

of acquiescing in what he considered unsound theology and an inadequate interpretation of history.[7]
We must remember that Ward was writing before
the Vatican Council definition. When the doctrine of
infallibility was finally proclaimed, it was completely
in accord with what Newman had always believed and
held.

Newman, whose intellectual honesty would not
allow him to agree with those he felt were extremists,
nevertheless understood the delicacy of his position.
He regretted, perhaps, the stern necessity of conscience which compelled him to take it, but he had no
thought of surrender. "The truth is," he wrote to a
friend in 1864, "there is a keen conflict going on just
now between two parties, one in the Church and one
out of it. And at such seasons extreme views alone
are in favour and a man who is not extravagant is
thought treacherous. I sometimes think of King Lear's
daughters and consider that they after all may be
found the truest who are in speech more measured." [8]

A second phase of Newman's character which had
marked repercussions on his manner of writing was
his love for England and for English things. He had
a perfect understanding of the English mentality,
probably because he shared it so completely. As Father

[7] Cf. Wilfrid Ward, *op. cit.*, II, 151, 212 f., 404.
[8] *Ibid.*, I, 572.

Michael Tynan remarks, he was an Englishman to his finger tips.[9]

In the *Eirenicon,* Dr. Pusey, treating especially of the devotion to the Blessed Virgin, had condemned as corruptions many of the devotional practices popular on the Continent. Newman, in the *Letter to Pusey,* pointed out that it was not the province of an Englishman to criticize devotions favored by other peoples, since he was necessarily incapable of understanding them from the viewpoint of other national mentalities. Expressing his personal taste, however, Newman wrote: "I prefer English habits of belief and devotion to foreign, from the same causes, and by the same right, which justifies foreigners in preferring their own." [10] Later on in the *Letter,* when Newman touches obliquely on the question of the propagation of Continental devotions in England, he indicates just how strong his English preferences are:

Now then we come to England itself, which, after all, in the matter of devotion, alone concerns you and me; for though doctrine is one and the same everywhere, devotions, as I have already said, are matters of the particular time and the particular country. I suppose we owe it to the national good sense, that English Catholics have been protected from the extravagances which are elsewhere to be found. And we owe it also to the wisdom and moderation of the Holy See,

[9] Cf. "The Approach to Newman" in *The Irish Ecclesiastical Record,* March, 1940, p. 263.
[10] *Diff.,* II, 20.

which, in giving us the pattern for our devotion, as well as the rule of our faith, has never indulged in those curiosities of thought which are both so attractive to undisciplined imaginations and so dangerous to grovelling hearts. In the case of our own common people I think such a forced style of devotion would be simply unintelligible; as to the educated, I doubt whether it can have more than an occasional or temporary influence. If the Catholic faith spreads in England, these peculiarities will not spread with it.[11]

Practically all Newman's writings demonstrate his understanding and love of the English character, with all its very real virtues, and in spite of its faults. In the original edition of the *Apologia* we find a summary of his feelings on this point: "I think, indeed, Englishmen the most suspicious and touchy of mankind; I think them unreasonable and unjust in their seasons of excitement; but I had rather be an Englishman (as in fact I am) than belong to any other race under heaven." [12]

Newman's intuitive comprehension of the English mind enabled him to avoid mistakes in dealing with it. He realized the Englishman's preoccupation with the tangible to the detriment of a taste for the metaphysical.[13] He is everywhere tactfully conscious of the similarity between the emotional tie which bound the average Protestant Englishman to his native coun-

11 *Ibid.*, II, 99 f.
12 *Apo.*, p. 38 (edit. 1865, New York: D. Appleton and Company).
13 Newman thus describes Hurrell Froude: "He had a keen insight into abstract truth; but he was an Englishman to the backbone in his severe adherence to the real and concrete" (*Apo.*, p. 24).

try and that which attached him to the Established Church.[14] The whole of the *Apologia* shows the skill which Newman could bring to bear in an appeal to the English sense of fair play.

The "Englishness" of Newman's style, so obviously a reflection of his own personality, did much to endear him even to those of his compatriots who did not share his religious convictions, and was an important factor in his success as a practical apologist. There is a remarkable passage in the *Letter to Pusey* which shows the subtlety with which Newman could appeal to the English mind. He is defending the devotion to the Blessed Virgin before a prospective jury of English readers, and this is what he writes:

I recollect the strange emotion which took by surprise men and women, young and old, when, at the Coronation of our present Queen, they gazed on the figure of one so like a child, so small, so tender, so shrinking, who had been exalted to so great an inheritance and so vast a rule, who was such a contrast in her own person to the solemn pageant which centered in her. Could it be otherwise with the spectators, if they had human affection? And did not the All-wise know the human heart when He took to Himself a Mother? did He not anticipate our emotion at the sight of such an exaltation in one so simple and so lowly? If He had not meant

[14] Belloc has an interesting comment on this aspect of the English Church in his Foreword to the Loyola University Press edition of the *Apologia*: "It is not a body of doctrine (it has never professed any body of doctrine with definition); it is a National Institution, exclusive of the Catholic Church and particularly of the central rite of the Mass because these are universal and not local. National feeling and the National Church were inextricably combined" (pp. ix f.).

her to exert that wonderful influence in His Church, which she has in the event exerted, I will use a bold word, He it is who has perverted us. If she is not to attract our homage, why did He make her solitary in her greatness amid His vast creation? If it be idolatry in us to let our affections respond to our faith, He would not have made her what she is, or He would not have told us that He had so made her; but, far from this, He has sent His Prophet to announce to us, "A Virgin shall conceive and bear a Son, and they shall call His name Emmanuel," and we have the same warrant for hailing her as God's Mother, as we have for adoring Him as God.[15]

How could Newman have better disarmed the English prejudice against Catholic devotion to a humble Virgin elevated by God to the pinnacle of all creation, than by reminding his English readers of their own emotions at the sight of the slender girl Victoria raised to the English throne? It is a comparison only an Englishman could have made, one which perhaps only an Englishman could fully appreciate.

It has not, of course, been the purpose of this chapter to present a complete, well-rounded picture of the character of Cardinal Newman. Our only wish has been to remind the reader that any appreciation of Newman's theological writings or evaluation of the criticisms directed against him must take into account two things: his complete intellectual honesty, and the sturdy English mold in which he cast the shining metal of his thought.

[15] *Diff.*, II, pp. 85 f.

SECTION II

The Principles of Interpretation

CHAPTER VI

THEIR NECESSITY

IF CARDINAL NEWMAN's theological thought is worth understanding at all, its value to the reader is in proportion to his comprehension rather than to his misinterpretation of it. Were it not for the systematic perversions to which Newman's theology has been subjected, such a remark would be almost self-evident. But Newman has been, and will no doubt continue to be, misinterpreted.

At least one well-known commentator is expressly in favor of such treatment. Charles Sarolea has written:

Catholicism of the future will certainly not be the miraculous and historical Catholicism of Newman, the eschatological Church of the early fathers. But Newman will nevertheless have contributed to the advent of the internal and eternal Gospel, because his disciples will have been able to deduce

from his works those conclusions which they do not contain. . . . The *plastic* mind of humanity will read into his
religious philosophy its own living thoughts, and the vitality
and influence of Newman will be in proportion as he is more
ingeniously misunderstood.[1]

It may be that we do Dr. Sarolea an injustice when
we find something almost humorous in the sentences
quoted. We are sure that their author took them very
seriously indeed. But even at the risk of appearing
hopelessly out of touch with the more subtle modes of
Newman interpretation, we must confess that to us
a misunderstanding, however "ingenious," is still a
misunderstanding—and certainly not a consummation
devoutly to be wished.

The present section of our study is devoted to the
examination of certain critical principles which must
be kept in mind in the study of Newman's theological
thought. These principles have an objective foundation in the facts of Newman's life, the peculiarities of
his genius, and the nature and form of his theological
writings. We believe that they are inevitable corol-
laries of the theology to which they are meant to be
applied.

There are elementary rules of good reading which
must be applied with equal urgency to the works of
any author. That an individual segment of an author's
thought should not be torn from its contextual circum-

[1] *Op. cit.*, p. 173.

ference and considered in an artificial isolation, for instance, is a universal principle of criticism. Obviously, if we choose individual sentences or expressions, or even sometimes page-length expositions, regardless of context, from almost any book ever written, we can make the author seem to say pretty much what we wish him to say. But Newman's works (as well as those of other authors) have been treated in this fashion, and not a few of the mistaken interpretations of the Cardinal's thought may be traced to this faulty procedure.

There comes to mind a recent example of the way a short selection from one of Newman's writings might give an incomplete and inadequate picture of his thought on a subject. In the small volume, *Bacon and Newman Bar God from Science*, Rev. Michael Hogan, S.J., protests that Newman, following Lord Bacon, utterly excludes God from science and grants to scientific endeavor and research a complete emancipation from the supernatural.[2] In Father Hogan's book a "single page" of Newman's *Idea of a University*[3] is advanced as the grounds for the condemnation of the Cardinal's opinions on a matter to which he devoted well over a hundred pages in the *Idea of a University* alone. This is rather peculiar in the light of the fact that the passage quoted is not a summary of

[2] Father Hogan's book was published in Jersey City, St. Peter's College Press, 1939.
[3] Pp. 221 f. in the edition we are using for this study.

Newman's views, but an exposition of what he considered Lord Bacon's reasons for postulating an opposition between theology and the physical sciences.

We regret that the scope of this study does not permit a detailed examination of the thirteen "false" categorical assertions which, according to James J. Walsh,
M.D., Ph.D., LL.D., the writer of the introduction to
Father Hogan's essay, are to be found on the one page
alone of Newman's *Idea*.[4] The capital fact which the
volume fails to stress is that Newman, while admitting
a certain degree of autonomy in the case of the physical
sciences, insisted that "Religious Truth is not only a
portion, but a condition of general knowledge." [5]
Newman never denied that God's Providence and
laws are the basis of all science; on the contrary, he
asserted it explicitly.[6] He maintained that, while separately each science is more or less an abstraction, if
we would have a complete view of the universe in the
concrete we cannot exclude any science, least of all
theology, the science of God.[7] To say that Newman
bars *God* from science because he insists on distinct
fields for theology *as a science* and for each of the
natural sciences, seems to us far from a legitimate conclusion.

We believe that it is sufficient simply to call to the

[4] Cf. Hogan, *op. cit.*, p. xlii.
[5] *Idea*, p. 70.
[6] *Ibid.*, pp. 63 f.
[7] Cf. *ibid.*, pp. 59 f., 214 f.

reader's attention the elementary truth that the rules of good reading must not be neglected in the perusal of Newman's works. The principles of interpretation to which this study is devoted are those which are *particularly necessary to the interpretation of Newman because of the factors we have indicated in our first five chapters*.

It seems hardly necessary to remark, in closing this chapter, that *every* erroneous criticism of Newman cannot be reduced to a failure to observe one or more of the four special principles we shall present. We believe that most of them can be so reduced; but the possible causes of error are multiple, and would admit of an indefinite catalogue. A critic of Newman may, for instance, fail to grasp an essential distinction, or to see the force of a chain of reasoning which, if appreciated, would obviate his objection. We shall indicate certain examples of this sort of misconception in the criticisms examined in Part Two of this study.

CHAPTER VII

THE FIRST PRINCIPLE

OUR summary of Newman's life has shown us that it was divided into two almost equal periods, Anglican and Catholic; and that the Anglican period had in itself several distinct phases, ranging from an initial outspoken intolerance with regard to Catholicism to the period of tolerance and understanding which immediately preceded Newman's reception into the Church.

This division of Newman's life has considerable importance for the student of Newman's theology. The works of Cardinal Newman, as we have them in the uniform edition, are comprised of writings from every period of his life. His final views on religious questions are, naturally, related in the books that he wrote as a Catholic. But his Anglican works contain much that is important intellectually, and still more, perhaps, that is of spiritual value.

Fortunately Newman did not allow his misgivings as to the reaction of both Catholics and Protestants to dissuade him from the republication of his Anglican

works.[1] By reissuing them himself, he was able to indicate that he no longer approved some of his early
positions. A mere disavowal would have been useless; his early works would, after his death, have been
published in spite of it. He chose to re-edit them himself, with corrective notes. Speaking of his early published thought, he asks, in the Advertisement to the
Essays Critical and Historical, that "either no reprint
of it will be made hereafter, or that the reprint of his
first thoughts will in fairness be allowed to carry with
it a reprint of his second." [2]

The most evident inadequacies, premature judgments, and biased evaluations based upon prejudice,
which occur in Newman's early works, have thus been
noted and repudiated in his revised edition, which

[1] The *Parochial and Plain Sermons* were the first of Newman's
Anglican works to be republished. They were edited not by Newman
himself, but by W. J. Copeland, to whom Newman wrote, in 1873, a
letter which takes cognizance of the problems attendant on the re-
editing: "You have been of the greatest use to me in the matter of
the Sermons, and I only regret you have had so much trouble: but
you have not had it for nothing. Unless you had broken the ice, I
could have republished nothing which I wrote before 1845-6. The
English public would not have borne any alterations—and my own
people would have been scandalized had I made none. They mur-
mured a good deal at the new edition of the Sermons, as it was—but,
since you, not I, published them, nothing could be said about it. After
this beginning, I took courage to publish my Essay on Miracles, and
the *British Critic* Essays, uncorrected, but with notes corrective of
the text. This too made some disturbance, but very little. And then I
republished . . . my University Sermons; and then I went on to mix
Anglican and Catholic Essays together; and now I hear no criticism
on these measures at all—and I have even dedicated a volume of my
Historical Sketches, half of it written as an Anglican, to an Irish
Bishop" (Wilfrid Ward, *op. cit.*, II, 396).
[2] P. viii.

began to appear in 1870. So far, then, as serious dogmatic errors are concerned, Newman's Anglican
works have largely been corrected.

We must be careful, however, in reading these
works for the real value they possess, to keep always in
mind the religious state of Newman when he wrote
them. Their atmosphere is one of sincerity and deep
spirituality, but it is hardly Catholic. The tone and
spirit, subtle things enough; the delicate shades of
emphasis which create a mood rather than prove a
point; the choice of argument and even, we might
add, the manner of thinking; all these unmistakably
reflect the fact that their author was a member of the
English Church.

Equally important to a clear understanding of Newman's thought is the recognition on the part of the
reader that the intellectual treatment of certain problems, notably those of the grounds of belief and the
development of doctrine, which we shall consider
later in our study, is not fully matured in Newman's
earlier works. To quote, in a haphazard manner, sections from his Anglican works as "Newman's opinion"
on such or such a problem, is to risk, if not a dogmatic
falsification, at least an intellectual misrepresentation
of the Cardinal's thought. As F. A. D'Cruz remarks:

Cardinal Newman has written about forty volumes, a little
more than half of them during his Anglican career, when
it may be said he was going through his theological appren-

ticeship, when his views were unstable and were constantly changing. The remaining volumes were written when, as he puts it himself, he had "come into port after a rough sea", when after mature deliberation he had accepted the Catholic Church as the Oracle of Truth on earth, and as an instrument adapted by the mercy of the Creator, to preserve religion in this world and retain a knowledge of Himself and of the truths He had revealed, so definite and distinct as to be proof against the energy of human scepticism. To these volumes then we should go if we desire to have his well considered and settled views. This fact should always be borne in mind. Instead of which, quotations are made indiscriminately from his earlier works, and he is held responsible for much that he has subsequently repudiated.[3]

It is not difficult now to formulate what we shall call the first principle for the interpretation of Newman's writings: *A work of Cardinal Newman must always be interpreted and judged in the light of the particular phase of religious and intellectual development during which it was written, and his later and more mature views on a question must be preferred to the earlier.*

[3] *Cardinal Newman, His Place in Religion and in Literature* (Madras, India: "Good Pastor" Press), pp. 4 f. (This book is undated. It lists in the Appendix books published as late as 1934.)

CHAPTER VIII

THE SECOND PRINCIPLE

WE HAVE pointed out in the first section of this study that Newman wrote most frequently as a controversialist. We also remarked that for the understanding of one of Newman's works a knowledge of the circumstances which called it into being is indispensable. Even such volumes as the *Essay on the Development of Christian Doctrine* and the *Essay in Aid of a Grammar of Assent,* which seem at first view independent of any controversy, contain long sections having as their purpose the refutation of particular errors or objections.

It follows, then, that unless we appreciate precisely what Newman is trying to accomplish in one of his arguments or expositions, we are in danger of missing his point and also of forming a false idea of the opinions he held on the subject. We must remember that Newman adapted not only his argument, but the entire tone and language of his writings to the purpose he had in view. We must beware of mistaking for a positive opinion of Newman a mere concession made for the sake of narrowing down a discussion to a precise controversial apex.

In the *Letter to the Duke of Norfolk*,[1] there is a sentence that may serve us as an illustration of the necessity of knowing Newman's purpose in a particular bit of writing. It is a sentence selected because of its rather startling form, which makes it useful as a test case for the principle of interpretation we are here considering.

In 1874, the Hon. William E. Gladstone, annoyed at the defeat of the Irish University Bill by the votes of the Irish Members of Parliament (following the rejection of the measure by the Catholic bishops of Ireland), published a bitter attack on the Vatican Council decrees, which affected, he thought, the civil allegiance of the Catholics of all nations, including England. Of the Catholic Church he wrote: ". . . no one can become her convert without renouncing his moral and mental freedom, and placing his civil loyalty and duty at the mercy of another." [2] The pamphlet amounted to an assertion that no Catholic owing allegiance to an infallible pope could be at the same time a loyal subject of the Queen.

This was not a challenge to go unanswered, and the aging Dr. Newman had not lost his powers as a con-

---

[1] Regarding the *Letter to the Duke of Norfolk*, cf. Wilfrid Ward, *op. cit.*, Vol. II, 397–409; Butler, *op. cit.*, II, 88–106; Thureau-Dangin, *op. cit.*, Part III, pp. 155–85.

[2] Gladstone, *op. cit.*, p. 6.

troversialist. His reply to the charges of the former Prime Minister was published as a *Letter to the Duke of Norfolk*. The *Letter* is a masterpiece of controversial writing. Newman neglected no circumstance which might aid the presentation of his case before the English public; it was not an accident that he addressed his *Letter* to the Duke of Norfolk, hereditary Earl Marshal of England and head of an ancient family distinguished alike for its loyalty to the Catholic Church and for its faithful service of the English Crown. Of the many Catholic answers to Gladstone's aspersions, Newman's alone "still lives and is read as a substantive piece of Catholic apologetics." [3]

The sentence of the *Letter* that particularly interests us here is the one with which Newman concluded his chapter on "Conscience." "Certainly," he wrote, "if I am obliged to bring religion into after-dinner toasts, (which indeed does not seem quite the thing) I shall drink,—to the Pope, if you please,—still, to Conscience first, and to the Pope afterwards." [4] It seems from this sentence that Dr. Newman, writing on the infallibility of the pope, minimizes that infallibility by asserting the primacy of conscience. An admission "of the greatest importance to the vindication of my argument," Mr. Gladstone wrote later. [5]

[3] Butler, *op. cit.*, II, 100.
[4] *Diff.*, II, 261.
[5] *Vaticanism: an Answer to Reproofs and Replies* (New York: Harper and Brothers, 1875), p. 10.

We must admit that to the Catholic reader even now this sentence is somewhat of a shock. Its real meaning and full controversial force are apparent only to those who consider Newman's purpose in writing it and the audience for which it was intended.

We must remember first of all that Newman was not writing a theological treatise on infallibility. He was answering Mr. Gladstone's strictures against the loyalty of the Catholic subjects of the Queen. In his introductory remarks, Newman had made this clear:

> The main question which Mr. Gladstone has started I consider to be this:—can Catholics be trustworthy subjects of the State? has not a foreign Power a hold over their consciences such, that it may at any time be used to the serious perplexity and injury of the civil government under which they live? . . . what I propose to do is this . . . to confine myself for the most part to what he principally insists upon, that Catholics, if they act consistently with their principles, cannot be loyal subjects.[6]

In the chapter in which the sentence occurs, Newman is not dealing directly with infallibility at all. He is defending the freedom of a Catholic to serve his country according to his conscience. This freedom of conscience, Newman maintains, can never be in conflict with the infallibility of the pope, because conscience is not a judgment upon any speculative truth or abstract doctrine, but bears immediately on conduct, something to be done or not done, here and

[6] *Diff.*, II, 179 f.

now. Since conscience is a practical dictate, he argues: ". . . a collision is possible between it and the Pope's authority only when the Pope legislates, or gives particular orders, and the like. But a Pope is not infallible in his laws, nor in his commands, nor in his acts of state, nor in his administration, nor in his public policy." [7] Thus the meaning of this sentence becomes clear when we consider it in the light of Newman's purpose in writing. We find that it is merely the expression of the truth that a positive and clear dictate of a man's conscience regarding some act to be performed or omitted must be obeyed rather than an opposing precept of a human superior. This is a conclusion no less orthodox than that of St. Thomas Aquinas himself in the same matter.[8]

Granted that the doctrine expressed is acceptable, we are still faced with a possible objection to the *form* of the sentence. Why so striking an emphasis on "Con-

[7] *Ibid.*, p. 256. We should note that Newman is not minimizing the great authority of a particular order of the pope, even though it be not infallible. He is merely showing that the conscience of a Catholic in regard to civil duties and the infallibility of the pope are on separate, non-conflicting planes. As for the possibility that some particular legislative act of the pope might conflict with a Catholic's "civil conscience," Newman does not deny a purely speculative possibility, but he affirms very strongly his conviction that "it cannot possibly happen in fact" (p. 241).

[8] "The obligation of conscience has the force of a divine precept. . . . Therefore, since a divine precept is binding when it is contrary to the precept of a prelate, and has a greater binding force than such a precept, the bond of conscience is superior to the bond arising from the precept of a prelate, and conscience will bind in spite of the existence of a prelate's precept to the contrary" (*De veritate*, q. 17, a. 5).

science first" and "Pope afterwards"? Would such a tone be adopted by a Catholic entirely loyal to the Holy See? Referring to the argument of the chapter on Conscience, of which the sentence we are considering was Newman's final remark, Gladstone wrote, a trifle triumphantly: "I must confess that in this apology there is to me a strong, undeniable, smack of Protestantism." [9]

The answer is simply that Newman wrote as he did because of the readers for whom his work was intended. He was not writing to convince loyal Catholics. His purpose was to assure Protestant Englishmen, ignorant of and consequently suspicious of the extent of the submission owed by Catholics to the Holy See, that a Catholic could be loyal to the monarch as well as to the pope.

One of the foremost Newman scholars in America, Joseph J. Reilly, Ph.D., has given us a bit of thoroughly sound criticism of the sentence in question. Dr. Reilly's remarks deserve quotation for their manifestation of the manner in which the implicit application of a necessary critical principle illuminates not only Newman's meaning, but his controversial genius. Referring to Newman's *Letter to the Duke of Norfolk*, Dr. Reilly writes:

He made it plain that his primary desire in answering Gladstone at all was not to explain the doctrine as such (for others

[9] *Vaticanism* . . . , p. 50.

had already done that) but to vindicate the loyalty of Catholic Englishmen. He proclaimed that the duty of Catholics to render unto Caesar the things that are Caesar's could not conflict with Infallibility rightly understood, and he even dared to shock many of his coreligionists in a famous passage that, however hazardous, carried conviction to minds from which no tamer words could have won a hearing: "If I am obliged to bring religion into after-dinner toasts (which indeed does not seem quite the thing), I shall drink,—to the Pope if you please,—still, to conscience first, and to the Pope afterwards."

Perhaps the man in the street read no further in this pamphlet; he left the merits of the theological questions to subtler minds. He was satisfied that the writer of that sentence was of the same stuff as they who had defeated the Armada, swept Holland from the seas, and won the day at Trafalgar.[10]

The sentence which we have been considering is not a particularly important one as regards theological significance. But it does furnish us with an example of the way the true meaning and full controversial force of Newman's writing become clear only when we take into consideration the purpose he had in writing and the readers for whom the work was intended.

The necessity of reading Newman's theological writings in this manner is clearly the underlying consideration in the comment of Joseph Husslein, S.J., on Newman's sermons:

But here as elsewhere we must bear in mind that as a preacher in the pulpit Newman invariably addressed himself

[10] "Newman as a Controversialist," in *The Catholic World*, CXVII (1923), 301. This essay was reprinted as chapter 6 of Dr. Reilly's *Newman as a Man of Letters* (New York: Macmillan, 1932).

to a select group, men and women whom he believed to be living in the state of God's grace or desirous certainly so to live. It is perfection, therefore, rather than conversion which is the keynote of his message. He is not a John the Baptist, crying in the wilderness, but rather one who reverently follows in the path where the Son of Man already has made His entry.[11]

In the sermons, then, it was Newman's audience which determined the keynote of his message; and to the present-day reader of those sermons, the recognition of the type of listener to whom they were delivered is a necessary factor in the appreciation of the implications and applications of the doctrine they convey.

We have dwelt at some length upon this second principle because, from the fact that such a large portion of Newman's writing is of a controversial nature, it is often useful for the determination of the precise sense intended; and because, as we have already said, even when a work is not expressly controversial, as in the case of the *Essay in Aid of a Grammar of Assent*, Newman's purpose in writing must be understood before the force of the argument becomes clear. The principle may be summarized thus: *Any particular work of Cardinal Newman must always be interpreted and judged in the light of the precise purpose for which it was written and of the persons for whom it was intended.*

[11] William R. Lamm, S.M., *The Spiritual Legacy of Newman*, with a preface by Joseph Husslein, S.J. (Milwaukee: Bruce, 1934), p. xi.

CHAPTER IX

THE THIRD PRINCIPLE

Even after we have taken into consideration, in the reading of one of Newman's works, the two principles outlined above, our correct understanding of Newman's thought is by no means automatically assured. There may remain intrinsic difficulties; that is, in the composition and verbal expression of the argument itself.

To Newman, writing was a fine art; or, perhaps more accurately, it was a craft. In the sense of conveying his thought clearly, his language is a masterpiece of precision. This is not to say that the English tongue itself is particularly precise, especially when employed in theology; it has too many meanings and shades of meaning for the same word. We must be certain, if we would grasp Newman's thought, that we know exactly what he means by the words he uses. Frequently recurring terms, such as "idea," "revelation," "probabilities," must be understood as Newman understood them. To attribute to them a meaning different from that which Newman intended is to falsify his entire argument.

Sometimes Newman defines a term early in the section of his work in which he employs it; but often it is only through an extremely careful reading of the context, and sometimes through recourse to parallel places in Newman's writings where the same word is used in a similar matter, that we grasp his exact meaning. This is not the quickest way to read Newman, or the easiest; but it is the only fair way. There are several misinterpretations and misunderstandings of Newman arising from a neglect of this caution. We shall consider some of them in the second part of this study.

Of course, if a commentator intentionally substitutes his own meaning for Newman's, the error is inexcusable. It is possible to use many of Newman's terms, as did the Modernists, and yet completely misrepresent his teaching; and no one has a right to link Newman's name with a false and subjective interpretation of his doctrine.

It seems paradoxical to say that theologians trained in the terminology and conventions of the Schools often have more difficulty in understanding Newman's theological thought than does the layman; but it is not far from the truth. Newman's nicety of expression, while a perfect vehicle for his thought, is seldom technically scholastic. A theologian whose preliminary formation included scholastic logic has, for instance, a clear idea of what he means by a "conditional proposition." But unless he is prepared to revise his definition while reading the *Grammar of Assent*, sections of that remarkable book will be irritatingly incomprehensible. By a "conditional proposition" Newman means a *conclusion* (of a syllogism, for example) which implies other propositions and its own dependence on them.[1]

To understand Newman, then, we must be prepared to accept his phraseology; only thus can we penetrate the ideas cloaked in terms unfamiliar to the theology of the Schools and appreciate the force of the argument of which these terms are the material.[2]

We have mentioned already the fact that Newman was not a systematic theologian. We should not read his works expecting to find a doctrinally complete and logically subordinated presentation of Catholic theology. Moreover, to isolate, on our own account, some of Newman's statements and erect upon them a "system" which is contrary to other portions of his teaching is hardly a contribution to the understanding of the Cardinal's thought. Of course, an obvious difficulty occurs. If, from certain of Newman's statements, a system can be built which contradicts other parts of his works, is not this merely a proof that New-

[1] Cf. *G.A.*, p. 2.
[2] Chapter ten, "Coming to Terms," of Mortimer Adler's *How to Read a Book* (New York: Simon and Schuster, 1940), has a particular value for the student of Newman.

man himself is illogical and inconsistent? The answer does not seem too difficult. Even apart from the fact that some of Newman's opinions are tentative, exploratory, and that others were later repudiated, we should not, in all justice, *postulate* inconsistencies, but should interpret an isolated section of Newman's works in accordance with the tenor of the whole. If our "system" contradicts some of his expressed, mature opinions, it is because the principle or principles on which we have constructed it were never intended to stand in artificial isolation as the basis of a system. Our logical concatenation of propositions has inferred from the original Newman *dicta* some independent, absolute meaning, which should have been qualified (and was, we presume, in Newman's mind) by other of his teachings.

Newman's works contain another pitfall for the unwary. His arguments, so often based partly on intuition, and abounding in subtle overtones and implications, can seldom be satisfactorily compressed into syllogistic form, and sometimes even an apparently valid reduction to conventional logical construction does them an injustice.

In *Bacon and Newman Bar God from Science*,[3] for example, the author quotes Newman as having written: "In other words, Physical Science, is, in a

[3] Cf. above, chap. 6.

certain sense, atheistic, for the very reason that it is
not Theology," [4] and proceeds to denounce this sentiment in the most decided terms:

> Of all the untrue and illogical pronouncements that Car-
> dinal Newman has made during his discussion of the present
> subject, this last is the most untrue and the most illogical. His
> present assertion is equivalently the disjunctive proposition
> that every science is either theological or atheistic. This is
> the hardest of the Cardinal's many hard sayings.[5]

Salva reverentia, we do not believe that the disjunctive proposition that "every science is either
theological or atheistic" is the equivalent of Cardinal
Newman's assertion. Nor would the syllogism em-
ploying as a major that disjunctive proposition lead to
a conclusion adequately expressing the sense of the
Cardinal's words.

An inspection of Newman's sentence shows us that
physical science is "atheistic," not flatly and without
qualification, but "in a certain sense." What is that
certain sense?—"for the very reason it is not theology." Now by "theology" Newman meant, in his
University lectures, the Science of God, or "the truths
we know about God put into system." [6] So Newman's

---

[4] Newman's sentence as found on p. 222 of the *Idea* is slightly different from Father Hogan's rendition of it. Newman wrote: "In other
words, physical science is in a certain sense atheistic, for the very
reason it is not theology." The sense, however, is the same in both
cases.

[5] Hogan, *op. cit.,* pp. 49 f.

[6] *Idea,* p. 61.

sentence means simply that a physical science is "atheistic" merely inasmuch as it is not "what we know about God put into system," but rather, for example, what we know about stars, or the crust of the earth, put into a system called astronomy, or geology.

Thus the sense of "atheistic" in Newman's sentence is extremely limited, conveying no positive denial of God, but merely expressing an abstraction necessitated by the specifying objects of the various sciences; whereas in our critic's disjunctive proposition "atheistic" is unqualified, with all its horrifying implications to the religious mind.[7] In other words, the shading of Newman's thought, expressed in his own way, has been lost in the brusque reduction to the truncated "disjunctive proposition" so dear to logicians.

We do not deny, of course, that Newman's sentence could be expressed in a disjunctive proposition adequately qualified; what we are trying to make clear is that Newman's thought very often cannot be "summarized in form." To convey Newman's meaning accurately and fully, the conventional logical form must frequently contain, at some length, an amplification of

---

[7] On p. 50 of his criticism, Father Hogan, holding that Newman also gives over to "atheism" such sciences of the spirit as psychology, remarks: "With the single exception of Theology, they are one and all atheistic to the extent of purposely ignoring the existence of God." This is a slightly more accurate recognition of what Newman meant by "atheistic" in the passage in question, but it is still unjust; "purposely ignoring the existence of God" is not so much Newman's thought as "not professedly treating, as a science, what we know of God."

Newman's words rather than a reduction to what might seem, after a cursory inspection, their "logical essentials." Otherwise we are likely to find that the probative value of Newman's argument has evaporated in the process of dessication.

In short, to read Newman's works from the standpoint of systematic theology, or scholastic terminology, or formal logical construction, is like trying to mold with our fingers a ball of quicksilver into a perfect cube. Our impression will almost inevitably be similar to that of the distinguished Roman theologian, Perrone, whose comment on Newman's *Prophetical Office* was "*Newman miscet et confundit omnia.*" [8]

We may now express our third principle: *Any particular work of Cardinal Newman must never be interpreted and judged as a work of systematic theology, or in the light of scholastic terminology or of conventional logical method, or with a meaning attached to the words different from that which Newman intended.*

[8] Cf. Wilfrid Ward, *op. cit.*, I, 18.

CHAPTER X

THE FOURTH PRINCIPLE

GIVEN a certain work, or section of a work, of Newman, the light thrown upon it by the three principles
we have already treated should aid us in understanding
its meaning and significance. The fourth and last principle we shall enumerate is also an aid to the understanding of Newman, but in a manner slightly different
from that of the first three.

We have mentioned more than once the importance
of interpreting a particular section of Newman's teachings in harmony with the tenor and trend of his
religious thought as a whole. At first, this may seem to
be a heavy task. Must we read all of Newman before
we can be reasonably sure that we understand a particular argument as he understood it and wished it to
be understood?

Happily, Newman himself has given us, with an
emphasis which renders them unmistakable and justifies our use of them as a norm of interpretation, the
basic ideas on which his conception of religion was
founded. As the reader will remember from our third

71

chapter, these two important truths are: the principle of dogma ("religion, as a mere sentiment, is to me a dream and a mockery"); and the principle of the existence of "a visible Church, with sacraments and rites which are the channels of invisible grace."

If we find, then, in the works of Newman, an isolated sentence or argument which, it seems, can be interpreted in a manner contradictory to one or both of these truths, we are led to a closer examination of the matter in question, in order to see if the contradiction is not more apparent than real.

We cite an example. The reader of the *Parochial and Plain Sermons* finds Newman speaking as follows:

> Common men see God at a distance; in their attempts to be religious they feebly guide themselves as by a distant light, and are obliged to calculate and search about for the path. But the long practiced Christian, who, through God's mercy, has brought God's presence near to him, the elect of God, in whom the Blessed Spirit dwells, he does not look out of doors for the traces of God; he is moved by God dwelling in him, and needs not but act on instinct.[1]

A Protestant or a Modernist, reading these sentences in the light of his own ideas of religion, and ignorant of the basic doctrines of Newman's religious thought, might construe them as a justification of an immanentist theory of Christianity. But the reader who remembers that for Newman "religion, as a mere sentiment, is . . . a dream and a mockery," is not inclined to

[1] Vol. I, p. 75.

find a glorification of the "religious sentiment" at the expense of objective dogma or the tenets of the visible Church. He understands Newman's words for what they are, an eloquent expression of the Catholic doctrine of the supernatural, supra-prudential inspiration of the Holy Spirit in the hearts of the children of God.

We must remember, further, that a good deal of Newman's early writing on religious problems is of a tentative nature. Sometimes he puts forth a hypothesis which he does not develop to its ultimate resolution because he himself has not yet established in his own mind the logical justification of such a resolution. The categorical profession, in the *Apologia,* of the truths of which we are speaking, is one of the factors rendering unjustifiable the action of a commentator in drawing, from Newman's statements, conclusions which Newman himself failed to draw, and of presenting these conclusions—which might be prejudicial to the expressed bases of Newman's conception of religion—as examples of Newman's thought.

Finally, if after a careful examination of one of Newman's particular arguments or expositions we still find it rather ambiguous and patient of more than one interpretation (and it would be strange indeed if we were not able to find, in forty volumes written without any obsession as to constant scientific theological precision of expression, at least a few such sections), it seems only elementary that such a particular part should be interpreted in accord with the whole of Newman's thought, rather than as contrary to it. And it will be found that the conditioning truths which we are speaking of in this chapter, together with the constant motive of the combat against Liberalism in religion, are not far from being an omnipresent leitmotiv in Newman's theological writings.

Our fourth principle, then, is an exterior criterion in the light of which we should view a given segment of Newman's religious thought. We do not believe that a careful application of the first three principles will leave a reader very often in doubt as to the scope and significance of one of Newman's developments. But if the case should arise, we can use the fourth principle somewhat as the biblical scholar makes use of the *analogia fidei* in explaining a seemingly obscure passage from the Scriptures. Only then can we be sure that we understand the argument as Newman understood it, or that we are using it as he intended that it be used.

We may phrase the fourth principle thus: *Any particular work of Newman must always be interpreted and judged in the light of the two doctrines which form the foundation of his idea of religion, the principle of dogma and the principle of the existence of a visible Church, with sacraments and rites that are the channels of invisible grace.*

CHAPTER XI

A METHOD OF READING NEWMAN

W E HAVE devoted the past four chapters to an exposition of the principles of interpretation which seem to us necessary for the understanding of Newman's theological thought. Naturally, we do not pretend that no one really comprehends Newman's teachings without the explicit application of the principles as such, one after another, to a given passage. We have attempted merely to systematize, in four rather dogmatically expressed formulas, the general background which the careful reader of Newman should have in mind during the perusal of his works, and which, we believe, the Newman commentaries which impress us as the most satisfactory have presupposed in a general way.

We have no intention of advocating a manner of reading Newman as mechanical as that employed by a student of cartography in reading a map. When, in this chapter concluding the first part of our study, we suggest the method of reading Newman's works which seems most rewarding to us, it is merely to indicate

one manner in which the background considerations
we have outlined in the form of four principles may be
applied in practice.

The first principle, stressing the importance of
knowing the period of Newman's life during which a
particular work was written, evidently requires a
knowledge of his life. There are many biographies of
Newman, but the most authoritative, the one which
has provided the source material for most of the others,
is *The Life of John Henry Cardinal Newman* by Wilfrid Ward. It is not, perhaps, the most "interestingly
written" of the biographies of Newman, but it is the
most complete. We advise the reading of this biographical study before a serious reading of Newman's
works.

It was with our first principle in mind that we ar-
ranged the list of Newman's works in the bibliography
at the end of this book according to the dates of composition and divided it according to the Anglican and
Catholic periods of Newman's life.

Still in connection with the first principle, the reader
of a Newman work should be careful to use the final,
revised edition. We have indicated in the bibliography
the date on which the definitive edition of each of
Newman's works appeared. The reprints dated from
that point on contain, as far as we know, the revised
text, unless the publishers indicate otherwise.

Many valuable clues to Newman's final thought on

a question may also be found in the *Index* to Newman's works compiled by Father Rickaby.[1] The importance of reading Newman's final thought on a
religious matter will be illustrated when we compare,
in the second part of this study, the two editions of
the *Essay on the Development of Christian Doctrine*
and the Oxford Sermon dealing with the same subject.

Personally we have only one exception to this rule
of reading Newman's works in their revised form.
We prefer the first edition of the *Apologia* because of
the matter it contains directly pertinent to the controversy with Kingsley, matter which was later omitted.
There is no question of doctrinal differences between
the first and the later form of the *Apologia;* but some
of Newman's most devastating controversial writing
occurs in his explicit answer to Kingsley's charges.
First editions of the *Apologia* are not too easy to ob-
tain, but there is a comparatively recent edition which
contains the material usually omitted.[2]

The reader familiar with the facts of Newman's life
is in possession of material indispensable for the application of the second principle we have treated—that
dealing with the necessity of knowing the purpose of
Newman in writing a particular work and the audi-

[1] Joseph Rickaby, S.J., *Index to the Works of John Henry Cardinal
Newman* (London: Longmans, Green and Co., 1914).
[2] *Newman's Apologia pro Vita Sua*, The Two Versions of 1864
and 1865, preceded by Newman's and Kingsley's pamphlets, with an
introduction by Wilfrid Ward (London: Henry Frowde, Oxford
University Press, 1913).

ence or class of readers for whom it was intended. To this end also, the introductory remarks with which Newman usually prefaces the volumes of his writings should be carefully consulted. And the *Apologia pro Vita Sua* as well as the two collections of the Cardinal's letters listed in the bibliography under the heading "Major Biographical Sources" will be found of the highest value.

The third principle we have outlined stresses the fact that we must accept a work of Newman for what it is, and on its own terms; that is, according to Newman's phraseology and method of composition, and in accordance with the sense in which he wished the words employed to be understood. As we have already stated in the chapter dealing with this principle, it entails a close examination of the work in question, in order to see if Newman expressly defines his terms, and, in case of doubt, a recourse to parallel passages where the meaning may be clearer. (We might add that this case of doubtful meaning sometimes arises not so much from any ambiguity inherent in a passage of Newman as from a false, though cleverly presented, interpretation of the passage in a later commentary. The absolutely precise sense which Newman intended then becomes a matter of considerable importance.)

In practice there is no difficulty in the application of the fourth principle. The reader should merely keep in mind the truths on which Newman's idea of religion was based, so that he can interpret according to the fundamental doctrines of Newman's religious teaching a section which, if isolated, might be understood in a different sense.

We scarcely need mention that the principles we have stressed in this section are also helpful in the evaluation of the many interpretations of Newman's religious teachings, both those which are the work of commentators who were the Cardinal's contemporaries and those written after his death. It may not be inadvisable, however, to reiterate briefly a caution based upon our exposition of Newman's temperament in Chapter V. Criticisms of Newman written during his life were often composed from a viewpoint intensely partisan. We sometimes find prejudice against Newman's thought and personality where we would least expect it: in Francis W. Newman, for instance, whose recollections of his elder brother the Cardinal, written almost immediately after the latter's death, are so obviously biased and unfair to their subject that the present-day reader is never tempted to grant them the tribute of serious consideration.

It is not within the scope of this study to criticize in detail the multitude of books written around Newman's theology. Those which we found especially valuable in connection with the *Essay on Development* and the *Grammar of Assent* will be noted in the chapters devoted to those works.

PART TWO

The Development of Christian Doctrine and the Genesis of Belief

SECTION I

Newman's Theory of Development and Its Critics

CHAPTER XII

THE ESSAY ON THE DEVELOPMENT OF CHRISTIAN DOCTRINE

It is not our purpose in this section to enter into a detailed exposition of the various theories concerning the development of Christian doctrine. We are interested in the theory of development only as it was presented by John Henry Newman in his *Essay on Development* and in the famous sermon preached at Oxford on the feast of the Purification, 1843. Here, as in the following section dealing with the *Essay in Aid of a Grammar of Assent*, we shall be directly occupied with the principal criticisms of Newman's teaching, examined in the light of the principles of interpretation to which we devoted the first part of our study. We have chosen this negative method of procedure as best adapted to the double purpose we have in view: to determine whether a number of specific and serious criticisms of Newman have a sound basis in reality, and to develop what we believe to be the true meaning of Newman's teaching on the points in question.

The theory of the development of Christian doctrine was not the discovery of John Henry Newman. As Father Marin-Sola has pointed out in a detailed survey which the reader interested in the history of the question might profitably consult, there are traces of it in the writings of St. Irenaeus, Origen, St. Basil, St. Gregory Nazianzen, and St. Jerome; Vincent of Lerins advanced the theory to the point of originating the comparison with the developments of acorn into oak and child into man; St. Thomas Aquinas and the great Scholastics admitted the development of the implicit content of revelation into the explicit.[1]

How then can one speak of "Newman's theory," as if it were original with him? Mainly because the modern interest in the problem and the modern manner of treating it may be traced largely to Newman's work. He was the first to present a detailed scientific study of the problem, and the impact of his intuitive genius on the question of development presents his conclusions (arrived at independently as far as Newman was concerned, though others had found them

[1] Cf. F. Marin-Sola, O.P., *L'évolution homogène du dogme catholique*, 2d ed. (Paris: J. Gabalda, 1924), II, 127–211.

before him) in such a striking form that they seem an
original creation. His analogy between the development of doctrine and the progress of the vital idea in
the human mind opened up a new and provocative
aspect of the matter. His comparison of doctrinal development with the growth of a living organism was
delineated with such a penetrating delicacy of nuance
that there has been nothing to add to it since. From
Newman's time, according to Father Léonce de
Grandmaison, practically every Catholic writer on the
subject has referred to Newman's analyses and accepted at least some of his conclusions.[2]

It is not without justification, then, that the *Essay
on Development* has been characterized as "epoch-
making." [3] Its influence has not been limited to spe-
cialized works of Catholic theology, such as those of
Marin-Sola and De Grandmaison. Converts to Catholicism have testified to the persuasive force which
accompanies its argument,[4] and its power as a contro-

---

[2] Cf. *Le dogme chrétien,* 2d ed. (Paris: Gabriel Beauchesne, 1927),
p. 111.

[3] Cf. F. A. D'Cruz, *op. cit.,* pp. 80, 621. J. Tixeront writes: ". . .
there appeared in 1845 an epoch-making work, J. H. Newman's
Essay on the Development of Christian Doctrine. It is not a history
of dogma, but the introduction or preface to one, and is replete with
profound views and original perspectives" (*Histoire des dogmes,* 12th
ed. Paris: J. Gabalda et Fils, 1930), I, 16.

[4] Arnold Lunn, for example, was deeply impressed with the section
of the *Essay* which deals with the papal supremacy, and quotes from
it twice in *Now I See* (New York: Sheed and Ward, 1934), pp. 216,
244. The *Essay on Development* is listed by Selden Peabody Delaney
as one of the books which helped him become a convert, in *Why
Rome* (New York: Dial Press, 1935), p. 232.

versial instrument in the hands of Catholic apologists has been attested by its adoption on the part of authors of doctrinal vulgarizations aimed at convert-making.[5]

The *Essay on Development* has been attacked by Catholics as being too Protestant. It has been condemned by Protestants as being too Catholic—that is, as having been molded not as a scientific theory but to justify "Roman corruptions" or to glorify the idea of the Church's infallibility. The Modernists pretended to find in certain features of the theory of development a justification of their own antidogmatic heresy; and for most Catholics the praise of the Modernists casts a deeper shadow over the *Essay* than do the unfavorable criticisms from the other two sources.

In this chapter we will outline the argument of the *Essay*. Since Newman's thought is not easy to condense, we do not pretend that our summary is an adequate one. Its purpose is merely to furnish what may be necessary for understanding the force of the objections against Newman's theory. Our outline will follow the disposition of the *Essay* as revised by New-

[5] In *The Faith of Millions* (Huntington, Ind.: Our Sunday Visitor Press, 1938), pp. 155, 460, Rev. John A. O'Brien signifies his approval of Newman's theory and makes use of his illustrations. Rev. Bertrand L. Conway, C.S.P., speaking of the development of Christian doctrine, calls the Newman *Essay* "the classic treatise on the subject" in *The Question Box* (New York: The Paulist Press, 1929), p. 113. Maisie Ward and F. J. Sheed have included a study outline on the development of doctrine, citing Newman and drawing largely on his ideas, in their *Catholic Evidence Training Outlines* (London: Sheed and Ward, 4th ed., 1939), pp. 251–53.

man in 1878. This later arrangement differs considerably from that of the first edition. The matter is largely
the same, but there are a fair number of textual
changes, some of which are highly significant.

The theory of the development of Christian doctrine formulated by Newman in the *Essay* is "an
hypothesis to account for a difficulty." [6] Newman believed that the natural place to seek for the matter of
divine revelation is in the historically existing Church
and in the doctrines it teaches and has taught. But the
difficulty opposed by some writers to such a course
was this: they maintained that when they consulted
the documents and literature of Christianity in times
past, they found "its doctrines so variously represented,
and so inconsistently maintained by its professors"
that it was, in fact, useless to seek in history the matter
of divine revelation. As a result, they claimed, they
were forced "to fall back upon the Bible as the sole
source of Revelation, and upon their own personal
private judgment as the sole expounder of its doctrine." [7]

To Newman, this was not a valid argument. In the
introductory chapter of the *Essay on Development*
he summarizes his own view:

> . . . that the increase and expansion of the Christian Creed
> and Ritual, and the variations which have attended the process
> in the case of individual writers and Churches, are the neces-

[6] *Dev.,* p. 30.
[7] *Ibid.,* p. 6.

sary attendants on any philosophy or polity which takes possession of the intellect and heart, and has had any wide or extended dominion; that, from the nature of the human mind, time is necessary for the full comprehension and perfection of great ideas; and that the highest and most wonderful truths, though communicated to the world once for all by inspired teachers, could not be comprehended all at once by the recipients, but, as being received and transmitted by minds not inspired and through media which were human, have required only the longer time and deeper thought for their full elucidation.[8]

The argument of the *Essay* is divided into two parts, the first considering "Doctrinal Developments Viewed in Themselves," and the second, "Doctrinal Developments Viewed Relatively to Doctrinal Corruptions."

In part one, Newman treats first the development of ideas as such, pointing out that it is a characteristic of a great and vital idea to live in the minds of its recipients, to become "an active principle within them, leading them to an ever-new contemplation of itself, to an application of it in various directions, and a propagation of it on every side." [9] He then describes the various kinds of development: political, logical, historical, ethical, and "metaphysical," carefully explaining the sense in which he is using each adjective. A truth of Christianity, inasmuch as it is received in

[8] *Ibid.*, pp. 29 f.
[9] *Ibid.*, p. 36.

human minds as an idea, might follow one of the five sorts of development defined, in the course of a process during which the implicit content of the truth gradually becomes explicit.[10]

Newman next presents the antecedent argument in favor of such development in Christian doctrine, from the very nature of Christianity as a fact which is received in the human mind as an idea.[11] He stresses the need of an infallible authority to guide this process of development, arguing that "in proportion to the probability of true developments of doctrine and practice in the Divine Scheme, so is the probability also of the appointment in that scheme of an external authority to decide upon them, thereby separating them from the mass of mere human speculation, extravagance, corruption, and error, in and out of which they grow." [12]

Newman then cites several examples from ecclesiastical history of what he considers genuine developments, demonstrating that Catholic doctrine as now held is logically as well as historically the representative of the ancient faith, and that "modern Catholicism is nothing else but simply the legitimate growth and complement, that is, the natural and necessary development, of the doctrine of the early church, and

[10] Cf. *ibid.*, pp. 41–54.
[11] Cf. *ibid.*, p. 55.
[12] *Ibid.*, p. 78.

that its divine authority is included in the divinity of Christianity." [13]

In the second part of the *Essay*, Newman anticipates the objection that these intellectual developments, in one sense natural, might, however, be untrue to their original, "as diseases come of nature, yet are the destruction, or rather the negation of health." [14] In other words, is it not possible that Newman's "developments" are really corruptions?

Newman's response is to assign "certain characteristics of faithful developments," which none but faithful developments have, and the presence of which serves to distinguish them from corruptions. [15] The notes which he assigns to a genuine development are preservation of type, continuity of principles, power of assimilation, logical sequence, anticipation of its future, conservative action upon its past, and chronic vigor.

The rest of the *Essay* is devoted to the "application of these seven notes to the existing developments of Christian Doctrine," such as the doctrine of purgatory and devotion to the Blessed Virgin. These applications, which would take too long to summarize here, are capital examples of the skill and flexibility with which Newman could call into play, in an argument

[13] *Ibid.*, p. 169.
[14] *Ibid.*, p. 170.
[15] *Ibid.*

of positive theology, his vast resources of patristic and historical erudition.[16]

[16] Cf. *ibid.*, pp. 207–404. There is an excellent and complete summary of the *Essay on Development*, including a brief description of the various applications, in the article "Dogme" by E. Dublanchy, *D.T.C.*, Vol. IV, cols. 1630 f. James J. Byrne, in his "The Notion of Doctrinal Development in the Anglican Writings of J. H. Newman" (in *Sylloge excerptorum e dissertationibus ad gradum Doctoris in Sacra Theologia vel in Iure canonico consequendum conscriptis*, tomus IV, Annus academicus 1935–1936, Lovanii, Sumptibus Bibliothecae Universitatis, 1937), presents a survey of those sections of Newman's Anglican works in which he touches upon the subject of development. We recommend this work as a valuable guide to the various stages of Newman's thought on the matter, although we cannot always agree with Dr. Byrne's interpretation of Newman's statements.

CHAPTER XIII

THE CRITICISMS FROM CATHOLIC SOURCES

A. *The Question of Terminology*

When Newman arrived in Rome some months after his conversion, he found that the principle of development was admitted by the Roman theologians, but that there was by no means any prospect of unanimous approval of his *Essay*. This was not surprising in view of the fact that it was written in English, not in Latin, Italian, or French, the languages most familiar to the theologians of the Eternal City.[1] In a letter dated November 15, 1846, Newman explains the situation:

All I have heard about my book here has been from two professors, one dogmatic of the Collegio Romano, (Jesuits). They evidently have been influenced by the American opposition which is known in Rome; but what they say after all is not much. They admit the *principle* of development but say I have carried it too far, judging by bits translated for them.[2]

[1] Cf. Wilfrid Ward, *op. cit.*, I, 159, 160.
[2] *Ibid.*, p. 161. A week later, in a letter to the same friend, Newman complains: "The theologians of the Roman Church who are said to sway the theology of Rome are introducing *bits* (without having seen the whole book) *bits* of my Essay into their lecture to dissent from. This seems very absurd" (*ibid.*, p. 167).

The most serious basis for the Roman opposition was in the delicate matter of Newman's terminology. His use of "probabilities" and "probable arguments" in the *Essay* was interpreted as denying the capability of the human intellect of arriving at certainty in questions of religion.[3] The most influential of the Roman theologians, the Jesuit Perrone, seems to have understood Newman's expressions relative to new "dogmas" as the equivalent of saying that new truth had been added to that first revealed to the Church.[4]

As Catholic theologians, the Roman professors naturally defended the completeness of Christian revelation from the very beginning. But in understanding Newman as being opposed to such a view, they were, we believe, misled by his terminology. The present-day reader, with the complete works of Newman available, has ample material for the refutation of any aspersions on the orthodoxy of the fundamental doctrine expressed in the *Essay on Development*.

With regard to the word "probability," for example, we find that Newman used it according to a distinct meaning of his own. A "probable argument" to him was not one concerning which there was a founded fear of error; he used "probable" in contrast, not to *certain*, but to *demonstrative*. To him, a proof based on "probabilities" was a proof grounded in cu-

[3] Cf. *ibid.*, p. 163.
[4] Cf. *ibid.*, pp. 184 f.

mulative or circumstantial evidence, as opposed to one based on scientific and absolutely demonstrative logic. Either form of proof, he holds throughout all his works, could be the basis of certitude. In a letter of December 8, 1846, he wrote: "I find the Essay is accused of denying moral certainty and holding *with Hermes* we cannot get beyond probability in religious questions. This is far from my meaning. I use 'probable' in opposition to 'demonstrative' and moral certainty is a *state of mind*." [5]

Father Perrone's objection to Newman's terminology regarding new "dogmas" is most important. If Newman considered that developments in doctrine were new dogmas in no way included in the original divine revelation, then his theory is inadmissible. But evidently this is not the case; in those rare paragraphs in which Newman uses the word "dogma" he intends to signify simply the explicit expression of what had hitherto been implicitly received and believed in the original deposit of Christian revelation. He argues, for instance, in the *Essay on Development:*

From the first age of Christianity, its teaching looked towards those ecclesiastical dogmas, afterwards recognized and defined, with (as time went on) more or less determinate advance in the direction of them; till at length that advance became so pronounced, as to justify their definition and to bring it about, and to place them in the position of

[5] *Ibid.,* p. 168.

rightful interpretations and keys of the remains and the records in history of the teaching which had so terminated.[6]

When we consult, in Newman's other works, sections bearing on the development of doctrine, we find parallel passages which assert, in so many words, the same underlying conception of doctrinal progress:

It is well known that, though the creed of the Church has been one and the same from the beginning, yet it has been so deeply lodged in her bosom as to be held by individuals more or less implicitly, instead of being delivered from the first in those special statements, or what are called definitions, under which it is now presented to us, and which preclude mistake or ignorance. These definitions, which are but the expressions of portions of the one dogma which has ever been received by the Church, are the work of time; they have grown to their present shape and number in the course of eighteen centuries, under the exigency of successive events, such as heresies and the like, and they may of course receive still further additions as time goes on.[7]

To the Apostles the whole revelation was given, by the Church it is transmitted; no simply new truth has been given to us since St. John's death; the one office of the Church is to guard "that noble deposit" of truth, as St. Paul speaks to Timothy, which the Apostles bequeathed to her, in its fulness and integrity.[8]

Doctrines remain implicit till they are contravened; then they are stated in explicit form.[9]

[6] *Dev.*, p. 122.
[7] *Diff.*, I, 394 f.
[8] *Ibid.*, p. 327.
[9] *The Via Media*, I, 223, note 4 (added in 1877).

If we examine the *Essay*, then, in the light of the third principle, that is, accepting the phraseology as, judging from parallel places in his works, we believe Newman understood it, we find that it is simply an original and highly ingenious manner of presenting a strictly traditional Catholic doctrine. When Newman speaks of "additions" as the result of doctrinal development, he means only the explicit statement of doctrines already implicitly held, which is the traditional view expressed by theologians of unquestioned orthodoxy.[10]

[10] Cf. Franzelin, *Tractatus de divina traditione et Scriptura* (Rome: Marietti, 1870), thesis XXIII; Van Noort, *De fontibus revelationis* (Bussum in Hollandia, Sumptibus Societatis Editricis Anonymae, 1920), pp. 153–67; De Grandmaison, *op. cit.*, pp. 243, 249, 262.

Marin-Sola has devoted two large volumes chiefly to the affirmation and explanation, with continual reference to the Fathers and Doctors of the Church, of this development from implicit to explicit. Of Newman he writes: ". . . this imprecision in terms led Newman to speak of additions or of dogmatic assimilation, whereas, in his thought, he intended only homogeneous developments of the implicit content of the primitive deposit of revelation. This is the only evolution which dogma admits" (*op. cit.*, I, 352 f.).

Marin-Sola's work has been recognized as a clear and complete vindication of Newman's *Essay*: "The recent work of the Dominican, Francis Màrin-Sola, on *L'évolution homogène du dogme catholique* (Friburg, 1924), is heralded as one of the most able treatments of the subject which has occupied the minds of many distinguished theologians. Father Marin-Sola, while examining the various methods used to explain the problem, proves himself an ardent champion of Newman on the question, against accusations of Modernists and others. He shows clearly that Newman is not only orthodox but traditional as well, and that it is primarily necessary to understand his terminology. Though Newman speaks of assimilation, preservation, and addition, he means nothing else but what the Scholastics call *explicatio impliciti*. 'New dogmas' are not such objectively but explicitly" (Francis J. Friedel, S.M., *The Mariology of Cardinal Newman* [New York: Benziger Brothers, 1928], pp. 73 f., note 67).

B. *The Criticism of Orestes Brownson*

Probably the most outspoken of the Catholic critics of Newman's development theory was the militant American convert, Orestes Augustus Brownson. His review of the *Essay on Development,* which appeared in *Brownson's Quarterly Review* in July, 1846, is one of the most vigorous examples of his controversial style.[11]

To the Orestes Brownson of 1846, Newman's theory of development was completely objectionable, and he did not hesitate to say so. It was "essentially anticatholic and Protestant." Not only was it unnecessary to the defense of the Church, but "utterly repugnant to her claims to be the authoritative and infallible Church of God." [12]

This general condemnation of Newman's theory was supported in Brownson's articles by a lengthy criticism of certain details of the *Essay on Develop-*

[11] Cf. *Brownson's Quarterly Review*, III (1846), 342–68. Brownson returned to the attack in January, 1847, with a review of J. Spencer Northcote's *The Fourfold Difficulty of Anglicanism;* the mention of Northcote's book was only incidental to a long criticism of the *Essay on Development.* (Cf. *ibid.,* Vol. I, New Series [1847], pp. 39–86.)

There is a brief treatment of Brownson's criticism of Newman's theory of development in Theodore Maynard's *Orestes Brownson, Yankee, Radical, Catholic* (New York: The Macmillan Company, 1943), pp. 198–205. Doran Whalen gives a vivid account of Brownson's reaction on his first reading of Newman's *Essay* in her *Granite for God's House, the Life of Orestes Augustus Brownson* (New York: Sheed and Ward, 1941), pp. 310–21.

[12] *Brownson's Quarterly Review*, III, 346. In his second criticism, Brownson wrote that Newman's *Essay* was "essentially repugnant to Catholic faith and theology" (*ibid.,* Vol. I, New Series, p. 82).

ment. He maintained that Newman's treatment of Christianity as an *idea*, even though he asserted the objectivity of the revelation of which that idea was formed, was repugnant to its divinity; and that any admission of development in doctrine would destroy the authority of the original revealed truth.

Probably the most serious (in the sense of having the best apparent foundation) of Brownson's objections to Newman's teaching is his disagreement with the third mark which Newman had assigned to characterize a "true development," namely, the "power of assimilation." In the *Essay*, Newman had written:

> In the physical world, whatever has life is characterized by growth, so that in no respect to grow is to cease to live. It grows by taking into its own substance external materials; and this absorption or assimilation is completed when the materials appropriated come to belong to it or enter into its unity. . . . This analogy may be taken to illustrate certain peculiarities in the growth or development in ideas.[13]

This third characteristic struck Brownson as completely at variance with the correct idea of Catholic doctrine, and he wrote, in the section of his review criticizing Newman's seven tests: "The third, which implies development by assimilation or accretion, is fatal to the sufficiency of the original revelation, by necessarily implying that the developed idea con-

---

[13] *Dev.*, pp. 185 f. For his review, Brownson used the edition published in New York by D. Appleton and Co. in 1845. In this edition the lines quoted appear on page 40.

tains what was not in the idea as originally given." [14]

The question is whether Newman, in the section on "assimilation," really opened wide the gates to the interpretation of doctrinal development as an eclectic process whereby Christianity appropriated for itself various doctrines pre-existing in the pagan religions.

To discover what Newman meant by his note of "power of assimilation," we must (according to our first principle of interpretation) consult the definitive expression of his thought on the matter, which is contained in the edition of the *Essay on Development* as revised by Newman for republication in 1878.

Orestès Brownson may to a large extent be excused for having reached the conclusions which he did regarding this third note, because in the first edition of the *Essay*, the section is somewhat ambiguous, and it is, to our mind, only with the preface and additions to the later edition that Newman's meaning becomes quite clear.

In the reprint of the 1878 edition from which we are quoting, pages 380–82 contain several paragraphs that did not appear in the first edition. We do not mean to imply that Newman had revised his opinion under fire. The fact that the new edition merely explains more fully what he had held from the beginning is evident from the circumstance that the explanatory addition really antedates the first edition of the *Essay*,

[14] *Brownson's Quarterly Review*, III, 348.

being a quotation from one of a series of essays which Newman wrote for *The British Critic* during the years 1836–42.

Brownson, however, was not entirely justified in his condemnation of 1842. He began his criticism from a rather arbitrary point of view, introducing his detailed objections with the following limitation: "We waive, here, all considerations of this theory so far as it is intended to apply to Christian discipline and theology, and confine ourselves to it solely as applied to Christian doctrine." [15]

This distinction may be possible for the criticism of most of the *Essay*, but not for the "assimilation" section, where Newman speaks sometimes of doctrine and sometimes of devotional practices and rites, without indicating precisely to which of the three his remarks primarily apply. He gives, for example, as an instance of "assimilation," the adoption by the Church of certain features of cult and worship which had been used by the pagans.[16] Newman had warned his readers that the seven notes were of "varying cogency, independence and applicability." [17] It seems that the section on "assimilation" may be applied mainly to rites and practices.

It is clear, however, that Newman considered the

[15] *Ibid.*, III, 347.
[16] Cf. *Dev.*, p. 371.
[17] Cf. *ibid.*, p. 171.

characteristic of "power of assimilation" also applicable in a certain sense to the development of doctrine properly speaking. But this emphatically does not mean that he regarded doctrinal development as the result of a mere eclecticism on the part of the Church. The key to his real meaning is furnished by a sentence which appeared in the first edition of the *Essay* as well as in the later edition. "That an idea more readily coalesces with these ideas than with those," he wrote, "does not show that it has been unduly influenced, that is, corrupted by them, but that it has an antecedent affinity to them." [18] In the light of the additions to the 1878 version of the *Essay*, his meaning becomes unmistakable. In the preface he admits that perhaps his confidence in his view of doctrinal development has sometimes led him to be "careless and over-liberal in his concessions to Protestants of historical fact," and he adds:

If this be so anywhere, he begs the reader in such cases to understand him as speaking hypothetically, and in the sense of an *argumentum ad hominem* and *à fortiori*. Nor is such hypothetical reasoning out of place in a publication which is addressed, not to theologians, but to those who as yet are not even Catholics, and who, as they read history, would scoff at any defence of Catholic doctrine which did not go to the length of covering admissions in matters of fact as broad as those which are here ventured on.[19]

[18] *Ibid.*, p. 187 (1845 edit., pp. 40 f.).
[19] Cf. *ibid.*, p. viii.

Applying specifically to the section on "assimilation" our second principle of Newman interpretation ("for what class of readers is the argument intended?"), we find that it is intended as a reply to those who would eliminate from the Christian creed all that resembles beliefs pre-existing in the pagan theologies, those who "cast off all that they also find in Pharisee or heathen." Newman was of the view that the Church, "like Aaron's rod, devours the serpents of the magicians." [20] He maintained that an *apparent* eclecticism could be, instead, evidence of the divine wisdom and providential guidance of the Church:

"And wherever she went, in trouble or in triumph, still she was a living spirit, the mind and voice of the Most High; 'sitting in the midst of the doctors, both hearing them and asking them questions;' claiming to herself what they said rightly, correcting their errors, supplying their defects, completing their beginnings, expanding their surmises, and thus gradually by means of them enlarging the range and refining the sense of her own teaching." [21]

To put it briefly, Newman's theory of "assimilation" as applied to doctrine seems to us to mean simply that the Church, in its legitimate development, could recognize with its divinely guided wisdom certain vestiges of the *primitive revelation* existing in a corrupt form in the pagan religions, and that this recognition might suggest the true explicit form of some doctrine

[20] *Ibid.*, p. 382.
[21] *Ibid.*, p. 381.

already implicitly existing in the Christian revelation independently.[22]

With regard to the note of "power of assimilation," then, even if it is not an explanation for which we have any great affection, and even if we are inclined to think that Newman made too many factual concessions, when we examine the section from the viewpoint of the first two principles of interpretation outlined in this study we find that Newman is not guilty of an unfortunate and unorthodox adoption of the eclectic theory. We must realize that the concessions made by a controversialist for the sake of argument do not necessarily reflect his personal opinions, and we must recognize the "assimilation" passages for what they were meant to be, an *argumentum ad hominem* against those who held that the Church had formulated her body of doctrine merely by selecting various beliefs from the pagan religions. And, lest we allow this section to assume an undue importance in the general interpretation of Newman's theory, we must not forget that Newman, in spite of his use of such words as "additions" and "assimilations," considered possible only one form of development in doctrine—from implicit to explicit—which is admitted by the traditional interpretations of dogmatic progress.

The powerful and ruggedly honest intellect of Orestes Augustus Brownson later recognized and ad-

[22] Cf. *ibid.*, pp. 380 f.

mitted that the reviews of 1846 and 1847 were based on a misconception of what Newman really held. In 1864 Brownson wrote:

Faith, objectively considered, is infallible, and the Church is infallible, by the assistance of the Holy Ghost, in teaching and defining it. But the faith is to us practically as if it were not, save in so far as it is actively received and appropriated by our own minds. This, we presume, is what Dr. Newman meant when he said: Christianity came into the world a naked idea, which the mind develops or realizes by its own action. Now in realizing, in actively receiving and appropriating the Christian dogma, or the faith, our minds are not infallible. We never conceive it adequately, or take in explicitly all that is in it; and we may, and often do, under various aspects, even misconceive it. Here is, if we understand it, the basis of Dr. Newman's Essay, and if so, our objections to it were irrelevant, and though well founded, as against the argument we deduced from it, they are not as against that which the author held, and intended to set forth, and perhaps did set forth to the minds of all who admired his book. We have long suspected that we did him injustice, though we have not changed our own views of the soundness of the theology we opposed to him, or thought we were opposing to him. The fact is, his book was profounder than we supposed, and was designed to solve theological difficulties which we had not then encountered in our own intellectual life and experience. This acknowledgment, spontaneously made, we hope will be accepted by the illustrious convert and his friends, as some slight atonement for any injustice we may have done him or them, since whatever injustice we may have done was done unwittingly and unintentionally.[23]

[23] *Brownson's Quarterly Review*, Vol. I, National Series, no. 4 (October, 1864), p. 480.

This generous admission from the most noted and acute of the Catholic critics of the *Essay on Development* is, it seems to us, a satisfactory note on which to close our brief examination of the principal Catholic objections to Newman's theory.

CHAPTER XIV

THE CRITICISMS FROM PROTESTANT SOURCES

IT HAS long been the orthodox Protestant contention that Catholic doctrine is *ipso facto* erroneous because it contains teachings not explicitly found in the letter of Sacred Scripture. James Martineau, one of the outstanding nineteenth century theological writers of the English Church, was quick to realize that the argument of the *Essay on Development*, if true, opens up a fatal breach in the Protestant position. In an outline of Newman's "theory of Christianity," Martineau thus assails the idea of doctrinal development:

On the mere Romanist appendages to this scheme,—the Invocation of saints, the Mariolatry, the Apostolic Succession, etc.—we mean to say nothing. They are chiefly remarkable for having raised up in their defence the obnoxious but highly important "doctrine of development." In the absence of any plausible support from Scripture, it became necessary, if they were to be retained at all, to widen the source of doctrine, and give an interpreting and determining power to the church.[1]

[1] *Essays Philosophical and Theological* (London: Trübner and Co., 1869), I, 361.

Of course, Newman's theory of development does not at all "widen the source" of doctrine. The Catholic Church has always held that no Catholic dogma, however lately defined, can contain anything which was not at least implicit in Scripture and tradition from the earliest ages of the Church. Newman's theory is merely an explanation of the manner in which a doctrine implicitly held from the first may become an explicit dogma of the faith. But we can agree with Martineau that for an orthodox Protestant the theory of development is definitely "obnoxious," because it shows how the definitions of the Church, far from being "corruptions" as Protestants maintain, are the inevitable manifestations of the divine riches of the original revelation.

Another Protestant critic who struck directly at a feature of Newman's theory which no Protestant could accept was the Principal of Mansfield College in Oxford, A. M. Fairbairn. Principal Fairbairn recognized that the theory of development as formulated by Newman was a powerful argument for that Church (and *only* for that Church) possessing an infallible doctrinal authority. After detailing Newman's tests of a true development, Fairbairn struck directly at what he considered the theory's weakest point:

This is an impressive apparatus for the determination of true developments from false, but the moment we attempt to apply the theory to history we are pulled up with a sudden shock. For it turns out to be a theory not for historical use, but for polemical or apologetical purposes. The developments are to proceed under the eye of "an external authority," which is to be the only and infallible judge as to whether they are true or false. But this remarkable provision calls for two remarks: first "infallibility" is not an "idea," but a very definite "institution," and so hardly conforms to the terms under which Christianity was said to have "come into the world"; and, secondly, to exempt "the infallibility of the Church" from the law of development is to withdraw from us the most flagrant example of its operation. If anything has a history which exhibits growth, it is this doctrine; to make one development the judge of the right or wrong of all the rest, is to mock us by refusing to enforce at the most critical point the law which has been so solemnly enacted. This may be expediency, but it is not justice; and injustice in history is no service to the cause of truth.[2]

Fairbairn's contention, in appearance quite plausible, need not delay us very long. He maintains that the doctrine of infallibility, in itself an example of the development of doctrine, should not be abstracted from the body of Catholic teaching and used to judge the other component doctrines. This argument is based on a misunderstanding of Newman's theory. Principal Fairbairn misses a major distinction: that between the fact of infallibility and the expression of the existence of that fact in a dogma of the Church.

It is not infallibility as a doctrine which guides the development of Christian doctrine; it is infallibility

[2] *The Place of Christ in Modern Theology*, 8th ed. (London: Hodder and Stoughton, 1898), pp. 33 f.

as an objective fact, existing as such from the very beginnings of the Church. The doctrine of the infallibility of the pope, for example, was not explicitly defined until 1870, but it existed implicitly in the deposit of revelation from the time of Christ. The fact that, until the Vatican Council, it was included only implicitly in the official body of Catholic doctrine which must be believed by every member of the Church does not mean that it did not really exist objectively from the origins of the Church. Infallibility, as an objective divine gift, could quite reasonably guide the development of doctrine (that is, the gradual becoming explicit of what was at first received only implicitly), including the development into an explicit formula of the doctrine of its own existence.[3] Newman, we must remember, did not maintain that the development of doctrine creates the realities it gradually makes explicit; it only recognizes ever more clearly their existence and their implicit presence in the original deposit of revelation.

If we search for the technical basis of Fairbairn's misunderstanding, it is to be found in the old familiar

[3] When we speak of doctrines only "implicitly" received in the early ages of the Church, we do not, of course, imply that the apostles themselves had a less perfect idea of the faith than did the doctors who followed them. It is the common teaching of theologians that the apostles had a divinely infused knowledge of the intrinsic sense of all the dogmas of the Church, although they did not propose those dogmas under all the forms in which they could be explicitly opposed to errors which were to come. Cf. Franzelin, *Tractatus de divina traditione et Scriptura* (Rome: Marietti, 1870), p. 247.

error of failing to interpret adequately the sense of Newman's terms; in this case, the words "idea" and "institution."

When Newman speaks of Christianity as an "idea" he does not deny the objectively existing reality of which the idea is conceived. "If Christianity," he writes in the *Essay*, "is a *fact*, and impresses an *idea* of itself on our minds and is a subject-matter of exercises of the reason, that idea will in course of time expand into a multitude of ideas, and aspects of ideas, connected and harmonious with one another, and in themselves determinate and immutable, as is the *objective fact itself* which is thus represented." [4]

When Newman speaks of an "institution" he does not mean simply an objectively existing reality, but an articulated and completely formed organization, explicitly and adequately recognized as such. Newman argued that the coming into the world of Christianity as "an idea rather than an institution" postulates the existence of an "authoritative sanction" to guide the development of that idea.[5] Therefore this "authoritative sanction" (the infallible authority of the Church) existed as a fact, which surely implies the existence of the Church itself from the beginning, as well as of its infallibility. Christ really founded the Church, outlining in substance the elements from

[4] *Dev.*, p. 55 (italics ours).
[5] Cf. *ibid.*, pp. 77 f.

which all future details of its organization were to be developed; but we may accept Newman's statement that Christianity did not come into the world as an "institution" in the sense that only in the course of time did it develop necessarily into the highly detailed organization, with its distinctly separate organs of disciplinary administration, its own jurisprudence, etc., which make it an "institution" in the sense which Newman intends.

If, like Principal Fairbairn, we were to insist on applying Newman's use of the word "institution" to the infallibility of the Church, we would be compelled to distinguish between infallibility as the fact existing from the beginning, and as the "institution," a term which could be applied (and then in an improper sense) only after infallibility had been explicitly recognized and defined, with its organs, limitations, and extension clearly determined. Thus infallibility did not come into the world as an "institution" in Newman's sense, but as a really existing attribute of the fact of Christianity, contained implicitly in the idea of Christianity.

It is rather a strange result of this theological controversy that the criticisms directed against Newman's theory by James Martineau and Principal Fairbairn should be remarkable principally for their indirect testimony to the value of the *Essay on Development* as an apologetic for Catholicism.

CHAPTER XV

NEWMAN'S THEORY OF DEVELOPMENT AND MODERNISM

A. *The Modernist Heresy*

The Modernist movement, which affected a large number of Catholic priests and laymen during the last years of the nineteenth century and the beginning of the twentieth, was a subtle one, difficult in the extreme to isolate and define. The writers infected with Modernism were careful not to present, in any one work, a clear-cut summary of their position. Their errors were scattered and partly concealed in a multitude of articles in religious and lay periodicals, as well as in volumes of theological vulgarization.

Almost without exception, the Modernists expressed an attachment to, and the highest respect for, the fundamental verities of Catholicism. At the same time, through designedly imprecise language and an almost diabolically clever indirect disparagement of Catholic dogmas, they undermined the very foundations of the traditional doctrine of the Church. It was a capital example of theological sabotage, a highly skillful "boring from within."

A great number of undoubtedly sincere Catholics were misled by the specious claims of the Modernist writers to be the modern interpreters of Catholic thought. The Holy See, however, was not deceived. In July, 1907, a decree of the Sacred Congregation of the Holy Office summarized and proscribed a large number of the subversive new doctrines, and in September of the same year Pope Pius X issued the encyclical *Pascendi dominici gregis*, which, in a remarkable achievement of synthesis, outlined and condemned the tenets of the Modernist heresy.

Although the papal document did not refer to specific works as containing particular doctrines, it was the mirror in which the Modernist leaders could not fail to perceive their image. Alfred Loisy recognized "two or three main sources" of the condemned teachings: his own works and those of George Tyrrell.[1]

The Catholic who seeks the true notion of Modernism as condemned by the Church has only to read the encyclical *Pascendi*. We feel, however, that we should outline at this point the salient features of the Modernist heresy, with the understanding that we do not claim to present a comprehensive summary of Modernism, but merely a few indications that will enable the reader of this study to appreciate the contrast between the heresy and the teachings of Newman.

[1] *Simples réflexions sur le decret du Saint-Office Lamentabili sane exitu et sur l'encyclique Pascendi dominici gregis* (Ceffonds [Haute-Marne], 1908), pp. 15, 17 f.

The foundation of the Modernist religious philosophy, as Pope Pius X pointed out, was an agnosticism which refused to allow that human reason could exceed the limits of sensible phenomena and ascend to a knowledge of even the existence of God.[2]

The Modernists explained the fact of religion by an immanent principle, a subconscious need which the human being feels for the supernatural, and which gives rise to what may be described as a religious sentiment.[3] This sentiment, or "religious sense," which springs from the dim depths of the subconscious by a process of vital immanence, is the seed from which all religion grows and the essence of all that any religion has contained or will contain.[4]

The human reason, examining the vital phenomena of this religious sense, translates them first into intellectual images, then into verbal expressions.[5] First, by a natural and spontaneous act, the intellect formulates a simple manner of expression, from which, by a process of deliberation, it develops secondary expressions, more clearly limited and more distinct. These secondary expressions, when sanctioned by the Church, become the dogmas of Catholicism.[6]

Thus a dogma is not an absolute, objective truth,

[2] *A.S.S.*, XL (1907), 596.
[3] *Ibid.*, pp. 597 f.
[4] *Ibid.*, p. 600.
[5] *Ibid.*, p. 601.
[6] *Ibid.*

but rather a mere inadequate symbol of its object, an instrument to be accommodated to the believer. Since a dogma is a symbol, an image, an instrument or vehicle of the truth, it must be adapted to man according to the exigencies of the religious sense. It must follow the changes and vicissitudes of man and his religious sense, and so is subject to a real, objective, and substantial evolution.[7] It is not necessary, precisely, to construct dogmatic formulas arbitrarily in the light of the exigencies of the religious sentiment. Their origin, number, and quality matter little enough. The important thing is that the religious sentiment, having modified the dogmas to suit itself, vitally "assimilates" them. Thus the primitive formulas must be accepted and sanctioned by the heart of man, and the development of the secondary formulas must take place under its influence.[8]

Our summary is, of course, an extreme simplification of the detailed exposition given in *Pascendi*, but we do not think that it is a misrepresentation of it. We can readily see how such a teaching, reducing the importance of dogma to a minimum, and making of it a continually fluctuating symbol, subject to a never-ending fluidity and to substantial changes in sense, cannot be reconciled with Catholic doctrine.

An attempt has been made to link Newman with the

[7] *Ibid.*, p. 602.
[8] *Ibid.*, p. 603.

Modernists on the strength of two of his theories, that of the development of doctrine and that which concerns the nature and force of the argument from probabilities. The argument from probabilities will be examined in the next section, when we treat of the *Grammar of Assent*. In this chapter we shall consider the question of Newman's theory of development in relation to Modernism as represented by its logical spokesmen, Alfred Loisy and George Tyrrell.[9]

It is, as a matter of fact, because Loisy and Tyrrell have all too frequently been called "disciples" of John Henry Newman and because the very association of their names with that of the Cardinal has served to cast a shadow, in some minds, upon the latter's orthodoxy, that we venture to touch upon the tangled problem of the relationship between Newman's teachings and the Modernist heresy. The difficulty of the ques-

---

[9] In a work which is considered one of the most complete and informative of the histories of Modernism, Jean Rivière stresses the important part played by Tyrrell: "Modernism was to find in G. Tyrrell one of its most exhaustive teachers, one of its most influential apostles, and one of its most resolute leaders" (*Le Modernisme dans l'Eglise*. Paris: Letouzey et Ané, 1929, p. 85).

The outstanding role played by Alfred Loisy in the heresy is too well known and universally admitted to need corroboration. We may add that Loisy himself would have been the last to protest at being considered a representative Modernist. M. J. Lagrange, O.P., remarks: "The epithet 'Modernist' has been very widely applied. Since the territory covered by the error was extremely broad, lacking precise limits, many were accused of Modernism who had no connection with it. But M. Loisy, on the contrary, was not in the least generous in his bestowal of the honor. Rather, he wondered whether the title of Modernist did not belong by right only to himself and George Tyrrell" (*M. Loisy et le Modernisme*. Juvisy: Editions du Cerf, 1932, p. 136).

tion has been referred to (with a noteworthy prudence) by the writer of the Introduction to the new French edition of the *Apologia:*

. . . the theology of Newman has, moreover, exercised an unexpected influence, through F. Von Hügel, in Modernist circles, especially in the case of George Tyrrell and Alfred Loisy. This is still a new subject, so delicate and controverted that I prefer simply to indicate its existence without going into it. To speak of it hastily would be to do so unjustly. But it is historically true that Modernism was one of the principal ways by which Newman was brought to the attention of the Continent and acquired fame there.[10]

Before comparing in detail the teachings of Loisy and Tyrrell on the question of development with those of Cardinal Newman, we have one observation to make: while it might be claimed (unjustly, we believe) that Newman held certain theories which paved the way for the Modernists, it is quite absurd to maintain, on the strength of this, that Newman was guilty of heresy.

In the first place, Newman wrote many years before the condemnation of Modernism, and even if he had held doctrines later condemned, we would have no more excuse for calling him a heretic than we would have for applying the same term to St. Thomas Aquinas because of his language which seemed to reject the Immaculate Conception, a doctrine which was several

---

[10] *Cardinal John Henry Newman, Apologia pro Vita Sua,* traduit de l'anglais par L. Michelin Delimoges, Introduction et notes par Maurice Nédoncelle (Paris: Bloud et Gay, 1939), p. lxviii.

centuries later to be defined as a dogma of the Church.

Secondly, Newman, whose whole-hearted submission to the Holy See was evident throughout his life, would have been the first to repudiate any of his teachings were they to be condemned by the Church. In the *Apologia* he wrote:

I believe the whole revealed dogma as taught by the Apostles, as committed by the Apostles to the Church, and as declared by the Church to me. I receive it, as it is infallibly interpreted by the authority to whom it is thus committed, and (implicitly) as it shall be, in like manner, further interpreted by that same authority till the end of time. I submit, moreover, to the universally received traditions of the Church, in which lies the matter of those new dogmatic definitions which are from time to time made, and which in all times are the clothing and the illustration of the Catholic dogma as already defined. And I submit myself to those other decisions of the Holy See, theological or not, through the organs which it has itself appointed, which, waiving the question of their infallibility, on the lowest ground come to me with a claim to be accepted and obeyed.[11]

Regarding his theory of development in particular, Newman's "advertisement to the first edition" of the *Essay* speaks for itself:

His [the Author's] first act on his conversion was to offer his Work for revision to the proper authorities; but the offer was declined on the ground that it was written and partly printed before he was a Catholic, and that it would come before the reader in a more persuasive form, if he read it as the author wrote it.

[11] *Apo.*, pp. 250 f.

It is scarcely necessary to add that he now submits every part of the book to the judgment of the Church, with whose doctrine, on the subjects of which he treats, he wishes all his thoughts to be coincident.[12]

One cannot help regretting that those Modernists who claimed to be Newman's disciples did not accept him as their master in his sincere and humble obedience to the Vicar of Christ and to all duly constituted ecclesiastical authority.

B. *The Theory of Development and Alfred Loisy*

In his *Mémoires pour servir à l'histoire religieuse de notre temps* as well as in his earlier writings, Alfred Loisy frequently refers to Cardinal Newman as having been of the same opinion as he, and of having influenced his writings.[13] But any resemblance between the two is purely superficial. As Marcel Chossat, S.J., remarks, the only similarity between M. Loisy and Cardinal Newman lies in the use by Loisy of Newman's phraseology, which had been made the fashion in France by Newman's "immanentist" admirers. In spite of Loisy's use of terms such as "life," "living faith," etc., which are often found in Newman, the identity is only verbal. Loisy changes the sense of Newman's terms to fit with his own preconceived ideas, just as he changed the sense of such words as

---

[12] *Dev.*, p. xi.
[13] Cf. *Mémoires* . . . (Paris: Emile Nourry, 1930), I, 410, 448, 473; II, 173, 414, 560. Cf. also *L'évangile et L'église* (Ceffonds [Haute-Marne], 4th ed., 1908), p. 203; and *Simples réflexions* . . . , pp. 64 f.

"faith," "revelation," "tradition," and "interpretation," from that accepted by the Church.[14]

From the summary of their teachings given at the beginning of this chapter, it may be readily seen why the evolution of dogma (in their own unorthodox sense) was a necessary doctrine of the Modernists. Like the others, Alfred Loisy tried to find a saving formula in the theory of development sponsored by the high intellect of John Henry Newman.

In the *Revue du clergé français* for December, 1898, Loisy, under one of his favorite pseudonyms, "A. Firmin," published an article devoted to "Christian Development according to Cardinal Newman." [15] Scattered through the pages of this early article (which is in many respects a fair reproduction of the argument of the *Essay on Development*) there are already distinct traces of an exaggeration of Newman's theory. These exaggerations are subtle enough, it is true, but they are sufficiently important to provoke the suspicion that Loisy is not so much presenting an objective exposition of Newman's theory as he is using Newman's terminology to clothe a less acceptable theory of his own.

We may illustrate this exaggeration of Newman's meaning by two significant examples. In justice to

[14] Cf. article "Modernisme," *D.A.F.C.*, Vol. III, col. 629.
[15] Cf. XVII, 5–20. For a summary of Loisy's theory of development, the reader may consult Léonce de Grandmaison, *op. cit.*, pp. 116–30; and *D.A.F.C.*, Vol. III, col. 624–37.

Loisy we must note that he does not pretend to be translating Newman word for word. But it is evident, both from the matter and expression of the sentences we shall cite, and from their position in Loisy's synthesis, that they are meant to parallel the words of Newman to which we shall compare them.

Loisy, in his article, places continual emphasis on the "transformation" of dogma. Where Newman says: "Here below to live is to change, and to be perfect is to have changed often," [16] the corresponding sentence in Loisy's analysis of the *Essay* is: "Ici-bas vivre c'est changer, et ce qui est devenu parfait ne l'a été qu'après bien des transformations." [17] When we translate Loisy as literally as possible we have the sentence: "Here below to live is to change, and that which has become perfect has done so only after many *transformations*."

That the difference is only a nuance, we admit; but it is of capital import as a reflection of the underlying thought of the two writers. Newman's use of the word "change" is much more applicable to the development of dogma in the orthodox sense than "transformation" is. A "change" may be only a slight modification, such as a clarification, but a "transformation" implies a basic, essential mutation, a metamorphosis, affecting the specific nature of the thing just transformed.

[16] *Dev.*, p. 40.
[17] *Revue du clergé français*, XVII, 6.

Roughly speaking, a thing may undergo a "change" and still be basically the same thing, but when we have a "transformation" one thing is "transformed" into another. The difference between the two words is substantially the same in French as it is in English.

Farther on in the same article, Loisy remarks: "Il est aisé de comprendre que le christianisme devait avoir un développement . . . parce qu'il était impossible, même pour les points de croyance les plus importants, de s'en tenir à la lettre de l'Écriture sans tomber dans un vain culte de formules." [18] Again translating Loisy's words literally, we have: "It is easy to understand that Christianity must have a development . . . because it was impossible, even for the most important points of belief, to adhere to the letter of Scripture without falling into a vain cult of formulas."

This sentence is obviously intended as a parallel of Newman's words: "And, indeed, when we turn to the consideration of particular doctrines on which Scripture lays the greatest stress, we shall see that it is absolutely impossible for them to remain in the mere letter of Scripture, if they are to be more than mere words, and to convey a definite idea to the recipient." [19] Newman, however, in the very next sen-

[18] *Ibid.*, p. 8.
[19] *Dev.*, p. 59.

tence, goes on to illustrate his meaning: "When it is declared that 'the Word became flesh,' three wide questions open upon us on the very announcement. What is meant by 'the Word,' what by 'flesh,' what by 'became'? The answers to these involve a process of investigation, and are developments." [20]

Thus Newman demands for his "development" only an explanation of what the words of Scripture mean. When he says that it is impossible to "remain in the mere letter of Scripture," he implies simply that it is impossible to be satisfied merely with words alone, without investigating the meaning they contain. Loisy, however, speaks of the impossibility of adhering "to the letter of Scripture"; he omits Newman's qualification of "mere" letter; and he seems to imply that, even if we thoroughly understand the meaning contained in this "letter," it is still insufficient; and the phrase which Loisy adds regarding a "vain cult of formulas" contains an overtone implicitly derogatory to the dogmatic formulas of the Church. We should remember, incidentally, that Newman's meaning must be judged in the light of his whole theory of religion, and that Loisy's meaning must be viewed according to *his* religious ideas which, in 1894, four years before he wrote this article, had already degenerated to a stage in which he had "lost the naïve

[20] *Ibid.*

faith of his youth and . . . only retained one article of the Apostles' Creed, *viz.*, that Jesus died under Pontius Pilate." [21]

We could examine other such parallel passages from Newman's original and Loisy's presentation of it and find a similar exaggeration of nuance, implying a different basic understanding of the theory of development. That we cannot point to any one categorical proof of this difference in the Loisy article under consideration, we readily grant; the Modernists were not in the habit of exposing their unorthodoxy too clearly. But the underlying tone and the cumulative effect of small exaggerations are convincing.

The passages we have examined from Loisy's article deal rather with doctrinal development considered as a process, abstracting from the starting and finishing points. When we advance a step further and examine not only the process involved in development but also the ideas of Loisy and of Newman concerning the original revelation from which development begins and the explicit dogma which is its consummation, it becomes obvious how complete the disagreement between their theories really is.

Newman, as we have seen, postulated as the source and beginning of the process of development the initial deposit of revealed truth committed to the

[21] A. C. Cotter, S.J., in *Theological Studies*, May, 1941, p. 244. Father Cotter's article is an excellent short summary of Loisy's life.

apostles. But Loisy denied this original deposit; rather than treat of the development of Christianity, he confused Christianity itself with its development:

Custodians and preachers of a living religion, the first followers of the Gospel did not for a moment think themselves bound in their teaching either by the letter of the formulas Christ had used, nor by the material reality of past events; they did not consider themselves the guardians of a doctrinal essence which Jesus never had the intention of preaching. . . . Jesus had been less the proponent of a doctrine than the initiator of a religious movement.[22]

According to Father Chossat, Newman, in admitting the initial Apostolic deposit of revealed truth, retains the essential element of any development; Loisy, far from presenting an acceptable solution to the problem of development, did not even propose it correctly, since he denied the initial revelation of the articles of faith.[23]

Regarding the *terminus ad quem* of doctrinal development, the defined truth, Loisy and Newman are also completely at odds. For Newman, the intellectual content of revealed and subsequently defined doctrine

[22] "Dépositaires et prédicateurs d'une religion vivante, les premiers adeptes de l'Evangile ne songèrent pas un instant qu'ils dûssent être liés dans leur enseignement, soit par la lettre des formules dont le Christ avait pu se servir, soit par la réalité matérielle des faits accomplis; ils ne se considéraient pas comme les gardiens d'une essence doctrinale que Jésus n'avait jamais eu l'intention de prêcher; . . . Jésus avait été beaucoup moins le représentant d'une doctrine que l'initiateur d'un mouvement religieux" (*Etudes évangéliques* [Paris: Alphonse Picard et Fils, 1902], p. xiii).

[23] Cf. article "Modernisme," *D.A.F.C.*, Vol. III, col. 629.

was of primary importance. For Loisy, the "value of dogmas" was "confined to their religious and moral signification." "That which constitutes revelation," he wrote, "is the spirit which animates beliefs whose material elements can be progressively and in a certain measure renewed without compromising the essential object, the necessary function of faith." [24] He would disregard the intellectual content of dogma, or at least reduce it to an absolute minimum of meaning, in favor of a vague conformity with the religious sense, or experience of the Christian conscience:

Dogmas are formulas of the traditional teaching, which have for their object to contribute to that work of religious and moral education which is the mission of the Church. These formulas are not immutable; they are perfectible. No dogma is a pure product of the imagination. All have responded to a need of the Christian conscience, and consequently contain a moral sense which we must extract when the symbol itself has become outmoded. [25]

[24] "L'idée de Tyrrell est parfaitement juste: la valeur des dogmes tient à leur signification religieuse et morale. Et j'ajouterai: ce qui fait la révélation, c'est l'esprit qui anime des croyances dont les éléments matériels peuvent se renouveler, en une certaine mesure et progressivement, sans compromettre l'objet essentiel, la fonction nécessaire de la foi" (*Quelques Lettres sur des questions actuelles et sur des événements récents* [Ceffonds (Haute-Marne), 1908], pp. 73 f.)

[25] "Les dogmes sont des formules d'enseignement traditionel qui ont pour objet de contribuer à cette œuvre d'éducation religieuse et morale, mission véritable de l'Eglise. Ces formules ne sont pas immuables; elles sont perfectibles. Aucun dogme n'est un pur produit de l'imagination. Tous ont répondu à un besoin de la conscience chrétienne, et conséquemment recèlent un sens moral qu'il s'agit d'extraire quand le symbol lui-même est frappé de caducité" (*ibid.*, p. 78).

So as to be certain not to exaggerate Loisy's meaning, we have translated "*caducité*" by the mild term "outmoded." Loisy might well have

We might summarize the relationship of Loisy's theory of development to Newman's in the following manner: first, Loisy exaggerates the extent and scope of development considered as process; secondly, Newman supposes the original deposit of revelation as the all-important prerequisite to development, while Loisy denies even the existence of this initial deposit; third, Loisy's teaching completely destroys the traditional idea of dogma, while to Newman dogma (and certainly not in Loisy's attenuated sense) was the fundamental principle of religion. Loisy does make considerable use of the Newman terminology, but his theory is not a portrait of Newman's. It is a caricature.

Those commentators who profess to have discovered a doctrinal kinship between Loisy and Newman have been misled, we believe, by a purely verbal similarity. They have failed to understand Newman's terms in the sense in which he used them, and have neglected to interpret isolated sections of Newman's works in harmony with the ensemble of Newman's thought and with the basic principles of his idea of religion.

This chapter is by no means a complete catalogue of the differences between Loisy and Newman. A thorough exposition would have to include numerous

---

intended the slightly figurative sense of the word, very common in French when used in connection with documents, rules, phrases of a will or testament, etc. In that sense, Loisy would have meant: "when the symbol itself has become *null and void*."

other points of divergence. Loisy, for instance, applied the theory of development to the actual revealed truths contained in the New as well as in the Old Testament, in an attempt to show that both of these two "collections" ("ces deux recueils") are the products of an historical evolution—an extension which even Loisy admits that Newman did not envision.[26] Loisy's teaching on the sacraments reduced their efficacy as well as their signification to a point so low as to destroy, to all intents and purposes, their supernatural value [27] —a theory which is diametrically opposed to Newman's postulate of "a visible Church with sacraments and rites which are the channels of invisible grace" as the second and necessary basis of his idea of religion.

C. The Theory of Development and George Tyrrell

According to an opinion expressed by Abbé Ernest Dimnet in one of his early works, it was George Tyrrell who best assimilated the spirit of Newman's doctrine.[28] Considering the whole of Tyrrell's teaching, and especially the way he interpreted Newman's theory of development, this is a judgment open to very serious criticism. One thing is certain: whether Tyrrell

[26] Cf. Mémoires . . . , I, 451; also Revue du clergé français, December, 1898, pp. 12 f.

[27] Cf. L'évangile et L'église, pp. 219–75.

[28] Cf. La pensée catholique dans L'Angleterre contemporaine (Paris: Victor Lecoffre, 1906), p. 131. Dimnet also refers to Tyrrell as a disciple of Newman on pages xxvi, xxviii, xxix.

did or did not penetrate the sense of Newman's theological thought, he did not adopt it as his own.

Tyrrell's theory of religion in its relation to dogma, as set forth in his volumes *Lex Orandi, Lex Credendi,* and *Through Scylla and Charybdis,* is enough to discredit entirely any claim that he was a disciple of Newman. Tyrrell's idea of religion and consequently his theory of development are conditioned by the peculiar sense which he attributes both to "revelation" and to "religion." To him revelation is primarily a religious experience, and only derivatively the record of that experience.[29] Religion is the "sense of, and the converse with, superhuman beings," resulting in doctrine only in so far as it gives birth to a "social organization" and a "constructive view of life." [30] The theologian, according to Tyrrell, should consider revelation "as a part of religious experience, by means of which he can, to some extent, reconstruct the whole of that experience." [31] If we say that theology is implicit in revelation, "it is not as one statement is implicit in another, but as theory is implicit in experience." [32] Theology is a "law" only in so far as it "formulates and justifies the devotion of the best

[29] Cf. *Through Scylla and Charybdis, or the Old Theology and the New* (London: Longmans, Green, and Co., 1907), p. 268.
[30] Tyrrell accepts Stade's definition to this effect in *ibid.,* p. 270.
[31] *Ibid.,* p. 284.
[32] *Ibid.,* p. 289.

Catholics, and as far as it is true to the life of faith and charity as actually lived." [33] While repudiating the out-and-out form of pragmatism which would reduce dogma to the status of a mere "ethical myth," Tyrrell proposes a theory which is hardly less prejudicial to the objective value of Catholic doctrine: insisting that a belief "which constantly and universally fosters spiritual life must so far be true to the realities of the spiritual world, and must therefore possess a representative as well as a practical value," he equally insists that "such representations are almost necessarily analogies or even symbols. And since there may be two analogies of the same truth, whose literal values are contradictory, it follows that the 'Law of Prayer' might easily give us very different creeds of just the same religious value—all equally true to the practical needs of the spirit-life, and analogously representative of the spiritual world." [34] It is inevitable that, with such postulates, Tyrrell's idea of dogma should clash with the constant teaching of the Church that its doctrines have an absolute and objective truth, independent of all accidents of time or place or circumstance.

George Tyrrell's presentation of Newman's theory of development is an extremely interesting one. He seems at one point to make use of the second principle

[33] Ibid., p. 105.
[34] Lex Credendi, a Sequel to Lex Orandi (London: Longmans, Green and Co., 1906), p. 252.

of interpretation we have outlined—and with somewhat surprising results. The examination of Tyrrell's
interpretation and the consideration of the arguments
against it necessitate a good many direct quotations
and some rather involved argumentation. We hope
that the reader will bear with us during the following
pages, for the very fact of its subjection to the searching light of Tyrrell's criticism only makes the true
meaning of Newman's theory stand out the more
clearly and distinctly.

In *Through Scylla and Charybdis*, Tyrrell has given
us his analysis of the two main portions of Newman's
works which treat of the theory of development. He
considers the Oxford University Sermon as being on
the side of the "new" or "liberal" theologians, who
discard "the fetters imposed on free thought by the
belief in a supernatural revelation and in a supernatural
interpretation of the same." The *Essay on Development*, Tyrrell maintains, was merely an attempt on
Newman's part to apply his theory (so far as it is applicable) to the history of Catholic theology.[35]

Tyrrell regards the "old" theology as that which
has for its principal object the "deposit of faith,"
understanding by that term "a certain body of divine
knowledge revealed supernaturally to the Apostles
and delivered by them under the form of certain categories, ideas, and images, to their immediate succes-

[35] Cf. *Through Scylla and Charybdis*, pp. 134, 145.

sors." [36] "That which is *semper idem*, constantly the same under all developments and accretions" is, in the case of the "old" theology as represented by the Scholastics, "a doctrine, a record of an experience gone, never to be repeated, preserved for us only in and through that doctrine." [37] And, because revelation is closed, "it is all important to preserve, if not the exact words, yet the exact sense and meaning which the record had for the minds of those to whom it was first delivered by the Apostles." [38]

To the "new" or "liberal" theology, on the other hand, the constant element is the "reality" dealt with, and not any doctrine or representation of that reality. The "new" theology is not bound to preserve any "deposit of faith": "It deals with those ever present evidences of God in Nature and in the universal religious experiences of mankind which are accessible to all, at all times, and by which all theories and doctrines as to the origin, nature, and end of these experiences can be experimentally tested." [39]

The two versions of dogmatic development will, then, necessarily be different: "The Church criticizes doctrinal developments by the standard of 'Apostolicity,' i.e., of their conformity to the sense of her original record, in respect to which they are either

[36] *Ibid.*, p. 112.
[37] *Ibid.*, pp. 113 f.
[38] *Ibid.*, p. 114.
[39] *Ibid.*

false or true. Her criterion of dogmatic truth is not the eternal reality, but the inspired representation of that reality given to her keeping by the Apostles." [40] The "liberal" theologian does not "ask or care that his theology be substantially identical with that of the past, but only that it be truer to experience than that which it supersedes." [41] Thus, in the case of the dominant theology of the Catholic Schools, the principle of development is but a "handmaid, an *ancilla theologiae*.[42] In "liberal" theology, the principle of development is "all-dominating." [43]

We may remark that Tyrrell, while he attempts to show that Newman personally was attached to the "new" or "liberal" school, maintains that he does not accept their doctrine himself. The theory which Tyrrell held at the time of writing *Through Scylla and Charybdis*, he says, "is a return to the earlier and stricter view as to the unchanging, unprogressive character of the apostolic revelation. It is a repudiation of all attempts to mitigate the supposed difficulties of this severer view by theories of development, dialectical or otherwise." [44] We must not be misled by this statement into believing that Tyrrell was inspired by any traditional respect for the "apostolic revela-

[40] *Ibid.*, p. 138.
[41] *Ibid.*, p. 136.
[42] *Ibid.*
[43] *Ibid.*, p. 135.
[44] *Ibid.*, p. 4.

tion." This revelation, according to him, does not admit of development mainly because revelation itself is a permanent phenomenon, given to every religious soul.[45] The religious man, therefore, has no need to be content with developments drawn out of the religious "experiences" of the apostles, which have no direct theological value.[46]

Tyrrell's interpretation of Newman's theory hinges on the meaning which he attaches to the word "idea" as used by the Cardinal. We must remember, he insists, "that with Newman 'idea' does not mean the mental formulation of an experienced object, but the object itself considered as apprehensible and intelligible. In his *Essay on Development*, he defines the 'idea' of an object as 'the sum-total of its possible aspects, or as we might say, the sum-total of possible experiences in regard to it; and as this sum-total is inexhaustible to the finite mind, it follows that we can go on for ever developing our formulation (or reasoned reconstruction) of the idea." [47] Tyrrell is dealing expressly with the University Sermon, but since he goes to the explanation contained in the *Essay* for what he considers support for his interpretation, he seems to be convinced that Newman used "idea" in his (Tyrrell's) sense in both works.

If Tyrrell's interpretation of the word "idea" is the

[45] Cf. *ibid.*, p. 292.
[46] Cf. *ibid.*, pp. 287-90.
[47] Cf. *ibid.*, p. 141.

true one, we must indeed view Newman's argument in a new light. When the Cardinal speaks of the development of the "idea" of Christianity, we must understand him as meaning, not the growth of our intellectual apprehension or representation of an immutable objective truth, but the growth, development, and change of the objective truth itself "considered as apprehensible and intelligible." Thus there would be a real and substantial mutation of the objective truth represented by the dogmas of the Church, and not merely an explicit recognition of what was implicit in the same objective truth from the beginning. This is, if true, an extremely serious objection to Newman's whole theory.

Newman, according to Tyrrell, defined the "idea" of an object as the "sum-total of its possible aspects." If Tyrrell's argument is to have any force at all, he must maintain that the "aspects" considered by Newman are aspects of the object itself as it exists in itself outside of the mind. (Tyrrell speaks, remember, of the object "as apprehensible," not as apprehended.)

In the *Essay*, the complete sentence from which Tyrrell quotes runs as follows: "The idea which represents an object or supposed object is commensurate with the sum total of its possible aspects, however they may vary in the separate consciousness of individuals; and in proportion to the variety of aspects under which it presents itself to various minds is its force

and depth, and the argument for its reality." [48] Here
Newman is unquestionably treating "aspect" as an
aspect of the idea, which is distinct (as existing in the
mind) from the object which exists outside it. His
"aspects" are the multiple parts of the same complex
mental representation. They are in the mind; although
naturally, if they are valid, they must *correspond to*
aspects of the external thing. It is worthy of note also
that Newman speaks of the "idea" as representing "an
object or supposed object." In other words, there can
be an "idea" of an object which does not really exist
—an idea which is merely subjective, with no basis in
external reality. Does not this argue to the fact that
Newman means by "idea" a mental representation, and
not the actual thing as it really exists outside of the
mind?

Newman uses the word "aspects" several times in
the passage from which this sentence is quoted, and
always in the sense of aspects of the idea in the mind,
never as externally existing aspects of the objective
thing of which the idea is formed. He writes, for example:

Of the judgments thus made, which become *aspects in
our minds* of the things which meet us, some are mere opinions which come and go. . . . Many of them attach to one
and the same *object*, which is thus variously *viewed, not
only by various minds, but by the same* . . . some, as being

[48] *Dev.*, p. 34.

actually incompatible with each other, are, one or other, falsely *associated in our minds* with their object, and in any case they may be *nothing more than ideas, which we mistake for things*.[49] . . . so also all the *aspects of an idea* are capable of coalition, and of a resolution into the *object* to which it belongs.[50]

It seems to us that Tyrrell, as well as Jean Guitton (who quotes Tyrrell on this point without comment) [51] unnecessarily complicates the Cardinal's thought. It is of course true, as Guitton points out,[52] that Newman, in different contexts, sometimes attaches different shades of meaning to the word "idea," as everyone who uses the English language does. But there is not a single instance in all of Newman, as far as we have been able to discover, which, upon a careful reading, gives any excuse for believing that Newman's "idea" was the thing itself as it exists outside the mind, or that there is any confusion between an "idea" and the object it represents. We might remark too, that the passages we have just cited, and which so clearly distinguish between the idea and its object, are from the opening paragraphs of Chapter I, Section I, of the *Essay*, where Newman is presumably explaining the notion of "idea" as it is to be understood in his treatise.

[49] *Dev.*, pp. 33 f. (italics ours).

[50] *Dev.*, p. 35 (italics ours). Cf. also *Dev.*, p. 55; and the refutation we have given above of A. M. Fairbairn's criticism of the *Essay* (chap. 14).

[51] Cf. *La philosophie de Newman* (Paris: Boivin et Cie., 1933), p. 82, note 1.

[52] Cf. *ibid.*, pp. 81 ff.

Newman, therefore, clearly distinguishes between the idea and the object of the idea. Tyrrell is guilty of violating the principle that we must accept and present Newman's terminology according to its meaning in Newman's context, not according to an arbitrary meaning of our own, which may falsify Newman's whole theory while retaining his words. Tyrrell's opinion notwithstanding, Newman does mean by "idea" the "mental formulation" of an experienced object, or rather (to escape from the ambiguity with which Tyrrell habitually uses the word "experience") of an object apprehended by the mind. And Newman's theory of development does not suppose the growth or development of the objective deposit of revelation, but only the development of the idea, received in finite minds, of this deposit which remains at all times objectively one and the same.

It seems to be Tyrrell's contention that of the two expressions of Newman's theory, the University Sermon, which "deals with the theory of doctrinal developments and not with its application to a particular controversy and its data," is more truly representative of Newman's own ideas than is the *Essay*, where Newman, according to Tyrrell, was merely arguing *ad hominem* against the Tractarians, and for that reason alone conceding their postulate of a *depositum fidei*.[53]

It seems that here Tyrrell is applying one of the very principles of interpretation we have been stress-

[53] Cf. *Through Scylla and Charybdis*, pp. 147, 151.

ing in our study: that we must view a particular work of Newman according to its purpose and intended audience. It remains to be seen whether his application is correctly made.

First of all, what are the differences between the two expressions of Newman's theory of development? Contrary to Tyrrell's insinuation, the Oxford Sermon, as well as the *Essay on Development*, supposes the original deposit of revealed truth, of which all doctrinal development is the explicitation.[54] Thus, as far as basic fundamental principles are concerned, the

---

[54] Speaking of the "formation of any Catholic dogma" and considering it as finally developed, "part answering to part, one, absolute, integral, indissoluble," Newman says in his Sermon: "And this world of thought is the expansion of a few words, uttered, as if casually, by the fishermen of Galilee" (*Oxford University Sermons*, p. 317). It would be hard to find a clearer indication that Newman regarded theological developments as having their origin in the original deposit of revelation transmitted by the apostles.

The Oxford Sermon presupposes also that doctrinal development is a process of explicitation of what has been implicitly received: "Now, here I observe, first of all, that, naturally as the inward idea of divine truth, such as has been described, passes into explicit form by the activity of our reflective powers, still such an actual delineation is not essential to its genuineness and perfection. A peasant may have such a true impression, yet be unable to give any intelligible account of it, as will easily be understood. But what is remarkable at first sight is this, that there is good reason for saying that the impression made upon the mind need not even be recognized by the parties possessing it. It is no proof that persons are not possessed, because they are not conscious, of an idea. Nothing is of more frequent occurrence, whether in things sensible or intellectual, than the existence of such unperceived impressions. . . . Now, it is important to insist on this circumstance, because it suggests the reality and permanence of inward knowledge, as distinct from explicit confession. The absence, or partial absence, or incompleteness of dogmatic statements is no proof of the absence of impressions or implicit judgments, in the mind of the Church. Even centuries might pass without the formal expression of a truth, which had been all along the secret life of millions of faithful souls" (*ibid.*, pp. 320 f., 323).

Oxford Sermon is no more "liberal" in Tyrrell's sense than is the *Essay* itself. But there are differences between the two, differences of method and detail. The Sermon is a rhetorical presentation of the main idea of development; the *Essay* is more in the nature of a scientific treatise. In the Sermon, Newman placed greater stress on the "symbolic" character of dogma than he did in the later *Essay*, especially in its final form, and he may thus be considered as implicitly admitting a greater latitude of change in the process of development.

In the Oxford Sermon, Newman wrote:

Creeds and dogmas live in the one idea which they are designed to express, and which alone is substantive; and are necessary only because the human mind cannot reflect upon that idea, except piecemeal, cannot use it in its oneness and entireness, nor without resolving it into a series of aspects and relations. And in matter of fact these expressions are never equivalent to it; we are able, indeed, to define the creations of our own minds, for they are what we make them and nothing else; but it were as easy to create what is real as to define it; and thus the Catholic dogmas are, after all, but symbols of a Divine fact, which, far from being compassed by those very propositions, would not be exhausted, nor fathomed, by a thousand.[55]

An objection then suggests itself to Newman. Since the idea of a supernatural object must itself be supernatural and hence above the powers of ordinary Christians, is it not possible that our anathemas, our

[55] *Ibid.*, pp. 331 f.

controversies, our sufferings, and our struggles are concerned merely with the poor ideas conveyed to us in certain figures of speech, and that we mistake words and names for things? [56] He answers, first, that divine grace might come to our aid by imparting ideas concerning the nature of God.[57] His second response is a comparison between our knowledge of God and of material things.

Again, the various terms and figures which are used in the doctrine of the Holy Trinity or of the Incarnation, surely may by their combination create ideas which will be altogether new, although they are still of an earthly character. And further, when it is said that such figures convey no knowledge of the Divine Nature itself, beyond those figures, whatever they are, it should be considered whether our senses can be proved to suggest any real idea of matter. All that we know, strictly speaking, is the existence of the impressions our senses make on us; and yet we scruple not to speak as if they conveyed to us the knowledge of material substances. Let, then, the Catholic dogmas, as such, be freely admitted to convey no true idea of Almighty God, but only an earthly one, gained from earthly figures, provided it be allowed, on the other hand, that the senses do not convey to us any true idea of matter, but only an idea commensurate with sensible impressions.[58]

In his development of this parallel, Newman seems at one point dangerously close to allowing a philosophical idealism:

[56] Cf. *ibid.*, pp. 338 f.
[57] Cf. *ibid.*, p. 339.
[58] *Ibid.*, pp. 339 f.

But what if the whole series of impressions, made on us through the senses, be, as I have already hinted, but a Divine economy suited to our need, and the token of realities distinct from themselves, and such as might be revealed to us, nay, more perfectly, by other senses, different from our existing ones as they from each other? What if the properties of matter, as we conceive of them, are merely relative to us, so that facts and events, which seem impossible when predicated concerning it in terms of those impressions, are impossible only in those terms, not in themselves,—impossible only because of the imperfection of the idea, which, in consequence of those impressions, we have conceived of material substances? If so, it would follow that the laws of physics, as we consider them, are themselves but generalizations of economical exhibitions, inferences from figure and shadow, and not more real than the phenomena from which they are drawn. Scripture, for instance, says that the sun moves and the earth is stationary; and science, that the earth moves, and the sun is comparatively at rest. How can we determine which of these opposite statements is the very truth, till we know what motion is? If our idea of motion be but an accidental result of our present senses, neither proposition is true, and both are true; neither true philosophically, both true for certain practical purposes in the system in which they are respectively found; and physical science will have no better meaning when it says that the earth moves, than plane astronomy when it says that the earth is still.[59]

Newman's solution of the problem is trust in God:

And should any one fear lest thoughts such as these should tend to a dreary and hopeless scepticism, let him take into account the Being and Providence of God, the Merciful and True; and he will at once be relieved of his anxiety. . . .

[59] *Ibid.*, pp. 347 f.

What is it to us whether the knowledge He gives us be greater or less, if it be He who gives it? What is it to us whether it be exact or vague, if He bids us trust it? What have we to care whether we are or are not given to divide substance from shadow, if He is training us heavenward by means of either? . . . We have an instinct within us, impelling us, we have external necessity forcing us, to trust our senses, and we may leave the question of their substantial truth for another world, "till the day break, and the shadows flee away." And what is true of reliance on our senses, is true of all the information which it has pleased God to vouchsafe to us, whether in nature or in grace.[60]

We have quoted these passages at such length because we wish, in the interests of truth, to present as fully as possible the section from Newman's writings which is the major foundation for the claim that he held a Symbolist view of dogma. We hope, however, that the citations given have conveyed also the *tentative and hypothetical tone* which characterizes this part of the Sermon. Newman is by no means laying down categorical principles. To use a rather inadequate expression, but one which best conveys the impression made upon our own mind, Newman seems to be toying with the idea of Symbolism rather than adopting it. The fact, too, that he is answering an objection, which lends an *ad hominem* character to the last three quotations, must not be overlooked.

Tyrrell, in his summary of the Sermon, entirely neglects the tentative nature of this section. He writes:

[60] *Ibid.*, pp. 348 f.

" 'The senses do not convey to us any true impression of matter, but only an idea commensurate with sensible impressions.' Of matter *in se* we know nothing, but only of matter as it impresses itself on the senses; of the Trinity *in se* we know nothing, but only of the impression which it makes on the human mind by its revealed presentment thereto. This 'impression' is not a verbal formula, but as real an experience as any sense-impression." [61]

Tyrrell's first sentence is a direct quotation from Newman, but it is a fragment of a sentence. On the grounds of his quotation, he draws categorical conclusions which are (should we be surprised?) entirely in accord with his "experience" prepossession. But if he had reproduced Newman's whole sentence, which, as we have seen above, is tentative, hypothetical, and in the nature of a retort, the weakness of his conclusions would have been instantly apparent.

If we accept the Oxford University Sermon as the definitive expression of Newman's thought, we may (only by stretching that expression, it is true, but still with some objective foundation) maintain that Newman regarded dogma as symbolic, a representation of reality in the manner that our external senses represent material things; and since Newman in the Sermon seems at least to entertain in some measure, however tentative, the thought that our external senses them-

[61] *Through Scylla and Charybdis*, p. 142.

selves may not truly represent reality, we are not completely assured that these symbols have a real objective foundation. Thus the way is opened for an extension of Newman's theory to permit a real substantial change in the meaning of these symbols, and hence a development which would be a transformist evolution of dogma.

Do not mistake our meaning. We do not think that this is the real, or even a legitimate, interpretation of the Oxford University Sermon. But we are trying to understand how the Modernists could claim to find a foundation for their theory of development in Newman's writings, and this is the only source we can discover.

When we consider Newman's works as a whole, however, even this nebulous foundation for the Modernist position vanishes.[62] From the citations we have already presented earlier in this chapter it is clear that Newman considered possible in the development of doctrine only the explicitation of what is already implicitly contained in the original deposit of revelation. It is noteworthy, also, that Newman expressly repudiated the theory of a real, substantial metamorphosis of doctrine. In the *Essays Critical and Historical*, in an essay which Newman wrote for the *British Critic* a short while before the preaching of the

---

[62] In a footnote to p. 139 of *Through Scylla and Charybdis*, Tyrrell admits: "I am only speaking of these two writings of Newman's considered apart from the context of his entire life and work."

Oxford Sermon, he gives tentative expression to a theory concerning the impossibility of finding a narrow, absolute, formal identity between the teachings of the Fathers and those of the churchmen of the nineteenth century, and the inevitability of a certain recasting of doctrinal expressions on account of the varying circumstances of the ages; but this theory he completely rejected in 1871, when he added the following note:

Of course it is true that the past never returns, and that reactions are always in one sense innovations. But what is said above goes further than this, further than I habitually went myself as an Anglican, and in my deliberate judgment. The hypothesis about the *depositum fidei* in which I gradually acquiesced was that of doctrinal development, or the evolution of doctrines out of certain original and fixed *dogmatic truths*, which were held inviolate from first to last, and the more firmly established and illustrated by the very process of enlargement; whereas here I have given utterance to a theory, not mine, of a certain *metamorphosis* and recasting of doctrines into new shapes,—"in nova mutatas corpora formas,"—those old and new shapes being foreign to each other, and connected only as symbolizing or realizing certain immutable but nebulous *principles*.[63]

[63] *Essays Critical and Historical*, p. 287. The question might be asked why Newman did not, in the later editions of the *Oxford University Sermons*, include a note repudiating any transformist interpretation of the section of the Sermon from which we have quoted in this chapter. We have indicated the answer. It is by no means certain that the Sermon legitimately lends itself to such an interpretation; and the fact that Newman did not bother to include a note clarifying his meaning is tacit testimony to the fact that he never for a moment suspected that the Modernists in years to come would seize upon the language of the Sermon and give it a tendentious interpreta-

In the final and definitive edition of the *Essay on Development* there is no mistaking Newman's meaning. He omits completely the vague expressions regarding the meaning and value of dogmatic formulas which had been present in the Oxford Sermon. This omission is a tacit but none the less significant repudiation of his early ambiguous words concerning the "symbolic" nature of dogma.[64]

---

tion which would cast doubt upon the firmness with which he held the traditional Catholic view of the significance of dogmatic formulas.

Incidentally, we might point out that Newman in his later years did not retain or reaffirm his earlier speculation about the possibility of physical reality being unknowable. In the *Grammar of Assent* he positively presupposed that we have a certain knowledge of physical truth. He replies to Chillingworth's objection that "there can be no rational assent to the Church's infallibility without some infallible means of knowing that she is infallible" with the retort: "What is this but to say that nothing in this world is certain but what is self-evident? that nothing can be absolutely proved? Can he really mean this? What then becomes of physical truth? of the discoveries in optics, chemistry, and electricity, or of the science of motion?" (*G.A.*, p. 227). It is worth remarking that the nature of motion was one of the very points on which Newman seemed to admit of doubt in the Oxford Sermon.

[64] It is true that Newman, in the first edition of the *Essay on Development*, cites a portion of the Oxford Sermon which ends with the sentences we have quoted previously in this chapter on page 140. "Creeds and dogmas . . . by a thousand." (The quotation in the *Essay* is on pages 31–32 of the edition published in New York by D. Appleton and Company, 1845.) But in the final and definitive edition of the *Essay*, that of 1878, Newman shortens the passage considerably. When reproducing the part of the quotation we have given on page 140, Newman leaves out the word "only" in the first sentence. More important, he omits completely the sentence: "And in matter of fact these expressions are never equivalent to it; we are able indeed, to define the creations of our own minds, for they are what we make them and nothing else; but it were as easy to create what is real as to define it; and thus the Catholic dogmas are, after all, but symbols of a Divine fact, which, far from being compassed by those very propositions, would not be exhausted, nor fathomed, by a thousand" (cf. *Dev.*, pp. 52 f.).

The question is: Can the more "liberal" Oxford Sermon (which the Abbé Dimnet, incidentally, calls "a beacon light of contemporary Catholic thought") [65] really be regarded as more representative of Newman's thought than the *Essay on Development?* It is a question which to our mind admits of only one answer: No.

The *Essay* is the expression of Newman's considered thought on the question of development. It is a scientific examination of the theory, whereas the

[65] The Abbé Dimnet, in an article published in the *Revue du clergé français*, XXXIV (1903), 234–48, preferred the Sermon to the *Essay*. After criticizing what he considered the "deficiencies" of the *Essay*, Dimnet wrote: "Because of these *lacunae*, the *Essay*, although sparkling with luminous thoughts, will soon be outdated. Happily, Newman had written, three years before his major treatise, an admirable sermon entitled The Theory of Developments in Religious Doctrine. These forty pages are a beacon light of contemporary Catholic thought" (cf. pp. 244 f.).

In mentioning the Abbé Dimnet in the same chapter with Tyrrell and Loisy, we do not mean to imply that Dimnet was a Modernist. But the facts are clear. The article in the *Revue du clergé français* unmistakably reflects, in spots, the spirit of Modernism which was so widely prevalent among French Catholic writers of the period. Together with several other essays, notably on George Tyrrell, this article was published in book form under the title *La pensée catholique dans l'Angleterre contemporaine* (Paris: Victor Lecoffre, 1906). The book expresses warm admiration for Tyrrell (". . . il est impossible de le lire sans l'aimer," p. 216), although in fairness to the Abbé Dimnet it must be noted that his praise of Tyrrell is based only on Tyrrell's early signed works, and not at all on the latter's publications under the pseudonyms "Hilaire Bourdon" and "Ernest Engles." Dimnet also accepts Tyrrell's theory of the tentative value of dogma only with reservations (cf. pp. 194 f.). In 1907, along with Modernist volumes written by Le Roy and Houtin, Dimnet's work was formally placed on the Index of forbidden books (cf. *A.S.S.*, XL, 1907). We believe that the Abbé Dimnet was personally loyal and submissive to the Church, but that he simply reflected in his volume the Modernist trend of thought current in France at the turn of the century.

Sermon is rather a rhetorical treatment, written from a devotional standpoint, and destined for the pulpit. In accordance with the first principle we have outlined, where Newman's later, more mature, more completely developed treatment of a question differs from his early and tentative references to it, we must accept the later work as representative of his thought.

Tyrrell's implication that the *Essay on Development* does not represent Newman's personal convictions because it was merely an *argumentum ad hominem* against the Tractarians, presupposing only for that reason the original deposit of doctrine, runs distinctly counter to the facts. Surely we have seen enough citations to convince us that the idea of a deposit of revelation, containing implicitly every future development, was not a concession for the sake of argument, but a positive belief of Newman himself, expressed in several of his works, and not only in the *Essay on Development*. Then too, Newman's research and deliberation in connection with the *Essay* was a determining point in his own conversion. Would he have been converted to Catholicism in writing a work whose underlying principle he did not admit, but only conceded for the sake of argument? The *Essay on Development* was also an attempt to express what Newman himself felt on the matter of development and on its influence in his attraction to Catholicism. In June, 1845, speaking of his forthcoming *Essay*, he wrote to

Mrs. William Froude: "Did I tell you I was preparing a book of some sort to advertise people how things stood with me? I think I am bound to do this, if I can —but you may so suppose, how difficult a thing it is to do." [66] A book which did not really represent Newman's own opinion would hardly "advertise people how things stood" with him. Finally, a prime concern of Newman's stay in Rome as a student at the Propaganda was his anxiety to have the theory of his *Essay on Development* (this was after it had been published) accepted by the Roman theologians, notably Perrone.[67] If this *Essay* did not really reflect Newman's own views on the important point of the existence of an original deposit of revelation, must we not attribute to him an insincerity which is at variance with everything we know of his character?

With Tyrrell's recognition of the principle that we must interpret a work of Newman in accordance with his purpose in writing and the audience to which it was destined, we have no quarrel, since it is precisely one of the principles of criticism which this study aims to establish and illustrate. But it goes without saying that such a principle should not be used in direct opposition to the objective facts of the case. It is one

[66] *Correspondence of John Henry Newman with John Keble and Others, 1839–1845,* edited at The Birmingham Oratory (London: Longmans, Green and Co., 1917), p. 378.
[67] Cf. Wilfrid Ward, *op. cit.,* pp. 156–75.

thing to recognize that Newman (as in the case of the "assimilation" section of the *Essay*) is speaking *ad hominem* and conceding points for the sake of argument, when we have valid reasons for so determining; it is quite another to dismiss a whole treatise as not representative of Newman's real opinion, when we have every positive and objective reason for believing that it is.

When Tyrrell, then, comments on Newman's theory of development, he misinterprets it on a variety of counts: he refuses to allow Newman's later thought to condition his earlier, a violation of the first principle of interpretation; he proposes a conception of the purpose of the *Essay* which is inadequate to the point of being completely false, a misapplication of the second principle; and he neglects to accept Newman's terms in Newman's sense, a violation of the third principle.

D. *Newman and the Modernists: Conclusion*

As we have seen, it is only by stretching a few loose and rather ambiguous expressions in Newman's Oxford Sermon that we can attribute to him any foreshadowing of the Modernist theory of development; but the foundations of even the Oxford Sermon can be reconciled with the traditional Catholic doctrine, and the ambiguous features were repudiated by Newman himself, either expressly in parallel passages from his works or by a pointed omission from his definitive treatment of the question.

Probably the best single general summary of the differences between Newman's theory of development and that of the Modernists has been given by the Most Reverend Edward Thomas O'Dwyer, bishop of Limerick, in a pamphlet published during the peak of the controversy occasioned by the publication of the encyclical *Pascendi:*

Newman's whole doctrine was not only different from that of the Modernists, but so contrary to it in essence and fundamental principle, that I cannot conceive how, by any implication, it could be involved in their condemnation. Nothing less than an explicit statement by the supreme authority of the Holy See would convince me to the contrary. I see no common ground in both systems. The word development is the only thing which they hold in common. They do not mean the same thing by Christianity, by dogma, by religion, by Church. They do not start from the same first principles, and consequently they are as separate as the poles.

Just see how the case stands. Newman starts with the revelation of the Christian faith by Christ our Lord. . . .

Consequently he holds that, whatever may be the processes of development with regard to that message, they are bound to it, and become a corruption if they change it. In other words, his theory is governed by the doctrine of the *depositum fidei*—the great body of truths which make up the complete system, if I may use the phrase, of the Christian faith. . . .

Now the whole scope and purpose of the *Essay on Devel-*

opment was to show that in the Church this original revelation has been preserved, that whatever definitions have been
pronounced, in the course of ages, they but declare author-
itatively, what it has contained from the beginning, and,
consequently, that the faith of every Catholic of the present
day is identical with that of the Church from the Apostolic
times. . . .

One may ask, then, what on earth has a theory such as
this to do with the views of these Modernists, which the
Pope condemns? They begin with no deposit of faith; they
do not admit any revelation in the Catholic sense; they deny
the existence of any body of objective truth, authenticated
for us by Divine revelation, as the source from which faith
has to draw its doctrines and the criterion by which all
human speculations as to faith are to be tested. With Newman the one question to be put to every proposition which
claimed to be accepted on Divine faith was, is it in the
primitive revelation? Does the infallible Church so teach?
But the Modernists put these questions on one side, as irrelevant, and ask instead, has this sentiment or feeling sprung
up in man's consciousness, having emerged from below its
threshold, and having been elaborated by the intellect, is it
for the time being, in accordance with the dominant belief
amongst the majority of the members of the Church? . . .

Surely it is an unwarrantable abuse, and deception to isolate a few conditions in one of these systems, and on the
strength of superficial, and mere verbal similarity to pretend
to find them in the other. Because Newman speaks of the
influence of the living thoughts and feelings of men who are
the recipients of Christ's revelation, we are not justified in
identifying him with those who repudiate his whole doctrine, because they harp upon the phrase that religion is
vital.[68]

[68] *Cardinal Newman and the Encyclical Pascendi Dominici Gregis*
(London: Longmans, Green, and Co., 1908), pp. 38–41. In this pam-

Catholic theologians who have touched upon the question are practically unanimous in denying, with Bishop O'Dwyer, the legitimacy of the Modernists' claim to depend on Cardinal Newman for their teaching.[69] But the absolute vindication of Newman, the

---

phlet, Bishop O'Dwyer shows that Newman's whole theology was, in its basic principles, opposed to the Modernist errors and in perfect harmony with the encyclical *Pascendi*. "As to what Newman would have thought of the system of the Modernists as a whole," he writes, "there can be little room for doubt. The entire fabric of his theology rested on the truth, which is elementary, that man by his intellect can know God, and can recognize a revelation, when proposed with due credentials, as coming from Him, and, consequently, he would have dealt very summarily with the Subjectivism which the Pope now condemns" (p. iii). Referring to the agnosticism which is a basic tenet of Modernism, Bishop O'Dwyer remarks: "Now it happens that, on almost every page of Newman's writings, we find the clear and unmistakable refutation of this shocking error. Newman held that God is the object directly of human science, and that this human science of God, and the first truth of all, that He exists lies at the very foundation of all religion" (p. 6). The pamphlet also stresses the essentially intellectual nature of Newman's religious philosophy, as contrasted with the "sentiment" of the Modernists. "If the system which these Modernists propound were a true representation, even in substance, of Christianity," Bishop O'Dwyer insists, "then Newman would not have been a Christian" (p. 19). Incidentally, the background of this pamphlet and the events leading up to its publication are interestingly described by Maisie Ward in *Insurrection versus Resurrection* (New York: Sheed and Ward, 1937), pp. 282–89.

[69] For instance, Marin-Sola and Schultes, O.P., who differ considerably on the question of the explanation of development in dogma and the emphasis to be placed on it, are agreed as far as the relationship of Newman's theory to Modernism is concerned. Marin-Sola maintains that a great injustice has been done to Newman, whether in pretending, with the Modernists, that he was the forerunner of their teachings, or in accusing him, as do certain Catholic theologians, of differing with Catholic doctrine merely because his terminology is not that of the Scholastics (cf. *op. cit.*, I, 351). Schultes, after a brief sketch of Newman's theory of development, concludes that the Modernists, it is certain, had no justification for twisting his doctrine to suit their own purposes (cf. *Introductio in historiam dogmatum* [Paris: P. Lethielleux, 1922], p. 291).

The only Catholic theologian we have read who seems to admit

authoritative answer to the charge that he can be suspected of Modernism, was written by Pope Pius X, the Pope who condemned the heresy. It is in the form of a letter he sent to Bishop O'Dwyer after the publication of the latter's pamphlet. This letter, which is not as well known as it should be, deserves, on account of its source and of its content, to be quoted at some length:

We wish to assure you that your pamphlet, in which you show that the writings of Cardinal Newman, far from differing with Our Encyclical Letter *Pascendi*, are in reality in closest accord with it, has our heartiest approval. You could not better have served both truth and the merit of the man. Apparently, among those whose errors we have condemned in Our Encyclical, there has been something in the nature of a pact that they should seek, in the sanction of Newman's illustrious name, approval of their own inventions. . . . You expose not only their insolence, but their artifice as well. For if, in the writings which antedated his conversion, there may perchance be something which has a certain similarity to some of the Modernist formulas, you rightly deny that the Modernists can find any support therein, because the thought behind the words and the purpose of their author are far different, and because Newman, on becoming a Catholic, submitted all his writings to the Church's authority for any correction which might be con-

some foundation, however slight, for the Modernists' claim is Alexius M. Lépicier, O.S.M., who remarks that Newman, always a most obedient son of the Church, would have abhorred the false conclusions which the Modernists, *if sometimes rightly*, most often falsely ("si quando per fas, saepissime per nefas") claim to derive from his works (cf. *De stabilitate et progressu dogmatis* [Rome: Desclee, 1910], pp. 15 f.).

sidered advisable. As to the many and important books he composed as a Catholic, it is hardly necessary to defend them against the charge of any kinship with heresy. For among the people of England, Newman in his writings always so served the cause of the Catholic faith that his works were alike of the greatest value to his countrymen and very highly regarded by Our predecessors. In such lofty esteem was he held that he was named Cardinal by Leo XIII, who was certainly a sagacious judge of men and affairs, and who held Newman deservedly most dear for all the rest of his life. Of course, in such a great number of works, something may be found which seems foreign to the traditional method of the theologians; but there is nothing which might serve to cast suspicion on his faith. You rightly affirm that it is not to be wondered at if, at a time when there were no apparent signs of the new heresy, Newman's manner of expression in certain passages did not display a special caution: but that the Modernists, in twisting these words to their own sense, contrary to the whole context, are guilty of falsity and deceit. . . . Would that they had really followed the authority of Newman, not that they might search his volumes in the light of their own preconceived ideas, in order to draw from them, with deliberate dishonesty, what they claim supports their opinions; but rather that they might adopt as their own the sincerity and integrity of Newman's principles, acquire his spirit, and follow his example.[70]

[70] Cf. *A.S.S.*, XLI (1908), 200–202.

SECTION II

Newman's Theory of Belief and Its Critics

CHAPTER XVI

THE ESSAY IN AID OF A GRAMMAR OF ASSENT

CARDINAL NEWMAN's second major contribution to theological literature, subordinate in importance only to his theory of development, was his analysis of the genesis of belief in the individual, outlined in the *Oxford University Sermons* and in the *Grammar of Assent*.

The ideas contained in both of these works are largely the same. The *Grammar* contains Newman's theory more fully and systematically outlined than was possible in a course of sermons. It is natural also that several points, rather hazily expressed in the *Sermons*, which were delivered in the years 1826 to 1843, should be given a more mature and clearer development in the *Grammar* of 1870. We must accept this latter work, then, in accordance with our first principle of criticism, as Newman's definitive thought on the matter, and base any evaluation of Newman's theory of belief on it rather than on the *University Sermons*. As a matter of fact, however, the reader of both works will find only minor accidental differences in the opinions expressed.

We maintained in our first chapter that Newman's theological writings were to a large extent conditioned by his ceaseless battle against the spirit of Liberalism in religion. The realization that the *Grammar of Assent* was no exception to this rule will help us to appreciate the argument it contains.

The *Grammar of Assent* may be regarded as directed against Locke's principle of certitude,[1] which, according to Sylvester Juergens, was "a basic truth for Liberalism." [2] Newman disagreed completely with Locke's pronouncement that the real lover of truth will not admit any proposition with greater assurance than will be warranted by the logical proofs on which it is built.[3] He believed that Locke had founded this doctrine on an "ideal of how the mind ought to act,

---

[1] This is apparent from an examination of Newman's conclusions in their opposition to those of Locke. The latter's theory is extensively examined in the *Grammar of Assent*. In Newman's opinion, Locke explicitly denied the value and validity of moral certitude even though he could not escape from admitting it implicitly. Cf. *G.A.*, pp. 160–81.

[2] Juergens, *op. cit.*, p. 4.

[3] Cf. *G.A.*, p. 162.

instead of interrogating human nature, as an existing thing, as it is found in the world." [4] He feared that it could be used as a rationalist battering-ram to attack the certitude which the average man, ignorant of scientific proofs, has for his faith in revealed religion.[5]

In this chapter we will consider briefly the main points of Newman's argument in the *Grammar of Assent*. Of all the works of Newman, not excepting the *Essay on Development*, the *Grammar of Assent* is the most difficult to summarize. We might almost as easily reduce to its "essentials" a landscape by Corot. Every detail, every tiny illustrative point we eliminate, turns out, to our surprise, to have been indispensable to the general effect. We will not attempt, then, to present a detailed summary of the *Grammar*, but will merely indicate (as we did in the case of the *Essay on Development*) the principal features of the theory it contains, in order that the objections we are to consider may not be unintelligible.[6]

---

[4] *G.A.*, p. 164.

[5] After calling attention to Locke's principle that doctrines are only so far to be considered true as they are logically demonstrated, Juergens adds: "The Liberals could therefore naturally challenge any Christian to either demonstrate his faith or be ready to abandon it, on the corollary, 'It is dishonest in a man to make an act of faith in what he had not brought home to him by actual proof.' A person therefore could not reasonably believe unless he could also *demonstrate* the reasonableness of that act. Evidently, then, the faith of most men is not according to reason, since but few can explicitly state the full grounds on which their faith rests. . . . The Liberals were of course quite disposed to admit that among the uneducated classes faith was but a mixture of prejudice and sentiment" (*op. cit.*, pp. 4 f.).

[6] The most satisfactory short summary of the *Grammar* we have

Two important distinctions are at the base of Newman's philosophy of belief. The first is between the two forms of assent, notional and real, and the second between assent and inference.

Newman begins, in the *Grammar of Assent*, by describing the various modes of holding propositions: the three mental acts of doubt, inference, and assent. Doubt is expressed by the interrogative form; the proposition asks a question. Inference, as an act, is expressed by a conclusion; and every conclusion is a "conditional" proposition because, from the very fact that it is a conclusion (e.g., of a syllogism), it implies other propositions and its own dependence on them. Assent is expressed by a categorical statement, which simply makes an assertion, and implies the absence of any condition or reservation of any kind, looking neither before nor behind, but being intrinsically complete.[7] It is with assent that Newman is mainly concerned.

Assent may be either "notional" or "real," depend-

---

found is that given by M. D'Arcy, S.J., in *The Nature of Belief* (London: Sheed and Ward, 1937), pp. 107-44. This summary does not include the final chapters of the *Grammar*. The section which Wilfrid Ward devotes to the *Grammar of Assent* is extremely well done (cf. *op. cit.*, II, 242-78). F. D'Cruz has a lengthy treatment of the main ideas of the *Grammar* simply expressed (cf. *op. cit.*, pp. 511-620).

It is hardly necessary to remark, we suppose, that the reading of any summary, however well done, is a poor substitute for a first-hand acquaintance with the richness of thought and depth of psychological analysis contained in the *Grammar of Assent* itself.

[7] Cf. *G.A.*, pp. 3-5.

ing on the way the proposition which is its object is apprehended. This distinction is best expressed in Newman's own words:

Now there are propositions, in which one or both of the terms are common nouns, as standing for what is abstract, general, and non-existing, such as "Man is an animal, some men are learned. . . ." These I shall call notional propositions, and the apprehension with which we infer or assent to them, notional.

And there are other propositions, which are composed of singular nouns, and of which the terms stand for things external to us, unit and individual, as "Philip was the father of Alexander," "the earth goes around the sun," . . . and these I shall call real propositions, and their apprehension real.[8]

Of these two modes of apprehending propositions, real is the "stronger," more vivid and forceful than is notional; because the experience of concrete facts is much more effective than an intellectual idea.[9] But the assent in both cases is unreserved and unconditional, an absolute adherence of the mind.[10]

Newman groups the assents to notional propositions under five headings, Profession, Credence, Opinion, Presumption, and Speculation. We may say, in general, that in its notional assents and in its inferences, the mind contemplates its own creations instead of things. In real assent, on the contrary, the mind is di-

[8] *Ibid.*, pp. 9 f.
[9] Cf. *ibid.*, pp. 11 f.
[10] Cf. *ibid.*, p. 16.

rected toward things, represented by the impressions which they have left on the imagination.[11]

Newman then applies his findings about assent and apprehension to the matter of religion. The introduction to this section is especially interesting:

> We are now able to determine what a dogma of faith is, and what it is to believe it. A dogma is a proposition; it stands for a notion or for a thing; and to believe it is to give the assent of the mind to it, as it stands for the one or for the other. To give a real assent to it is an act of religion; to give a notional, is a theological act. It is discerned, rested in, and appropriated as a reality, by the religious imagination; it is held as a truth, by the theological intellect.
>
> Not as if there were in fact, or could be, any line of demarcation or party-wall between these two modes of assent, the religious and the theological. As intellect is common to all men as well as imagination, every religious man is to a certain extent a theologian, and no theology can start or thrive without the initiative and abiding presence of religion. As in matters of this world, sense, sensation, instinct, intuition, supply us with facts, and the intellect uses them; so, as regards our relations with the Supreme Being, we get our facts from the witness, first of nature, then of revelation, and our doctrines, in which they issue, through the exercise of abstraction and inference. This is obvious; but it does not interfere with holding that there is a theological habit of mind, and a religious, each distinct from each, religion using theology, and theology using religion.[12]

The second part of the *Grammar* is devoted to a consideration of the relation between assent and in-

---

[11] Cf. *ibid.*, p. 75.
[12] *Ibid.*, pp. 98 f.

ference. Newman regards these as distinct acts of the mind. The act of assent is unconditional; whereas inference, which goes before assent, is conditional, and the unconditional acceptance of a proposition can be the result of its conditional verification. This last can be seen from a simple example: every man gives an absolute and unqualified assent to the proposition "I shall die," which is not and cannot be demonstrated by formal logic.[13]

Newman's theory is in direct contrast to that of philosophic authors such as Locke, who postulate degrees of assent, in proportion as the reasons for a proposition are strong or weak; and from whose theory it follows that "absolute assent has no legitimate exercise, except as ratifying acts of intuition or demonstration." Newman rejects this as an "a priori" theory, and appeals to the facts of human nature for illustrations of assents "which men give on evidence short of intuition and demonstration, yet which are as unconditional as if they had that highest evidence." [14]

The next distinction in the *Grammar* is that between simple assent, which is exercised unconsciously, and complex assent, which is made consciously and deliberately. We may aim at inferring a proposition, while all the time we assent to it; we may employ ourselves in proving what we already believe to be true,

13 Cf. *ibid.*, pp. 157 f.
14 *Ibid.*, pp. 159, 176.

simply, for example, in order to ascertain the producible evidence in its favor.[15] Thus, as the result of a reasoned investigation, we may give assent not only to a proposition, but also to the truth of that proposition. We give "an assent to an assent"—what is commonly called a conviction.[16] Such a conviction Newman calls a certitude, and the proposition, a certainty.[17]

Newman regards it as unquestionable that we have a real certitude regarding "the elements of knowledge, whether general, scientific, historical, or such as bear on our daily needs and habits, and relate to ourselves, our homes and families, our friends, neighbourhood, country, and civil state." [18] He is prepared, then, considering the non-demonstrability of the bases on which these certitudes rest, to call probability "the guide of life," if this saying is properly explained; that is, if we remember that without first principles there can be no conclusions at all, "and that thus probability does in some sense presuppose and require the existence of truths which are certain." [19]

The question is now carried further. Can such certitude be attributed to the state of mind with which the average man holds religious truth? Newman maintains that it can. "The initial truths of divine knowl-

[15] Cf. ibid., p. 191.
[16] Cf. ibid., p. 195.
[17] Cf. ibid., p. 196.
[18] Ibid., p. 236.
[19] Ibid., p. 237.

edge," he says, "ought to be viewed as parallel to the initial truths of secular: as the latter are certain, so too are the former." [20]

We can now consider more fully the relationship between inference and assent. Inference, as we have said, is conditional, depending on premises. And, Newman maintains, because it deals with the comparison of propositions, its conclusions are abstract, and can only be applied to concrete matters with probability.[21] Assent, however, is unconditional, and is applied unconditionally to the concrete. How can we pass from inference to assent? Newman replies that it is not formal logical sequence which enables us to become certain of what is concrete, but it is "the cumulation of probabilities, independent of each other, arising out of the nature and circumstances of the particular case which is under review; probabilities too fine to avail separately, too subtle and circuitous to be convertible into syllogisms, too numerous and various for such conversion, even were they convertible." [22] As an illustration of the way the converging probabilities are connected with the certain assent, Newman gives a brilliant analogy from the science of mathematics:

We know that a regular polygon, inscribed in a circle, its sides being continually diminished, tends to become that

[20] *Ibid.*
[21] Cf. *ibid.,* pp. 268 f.
[22] *Ibid.,* p. 288.

circle, as its limit; but it vanishes before it has coincided with the circle, so that its tendency to be the circle, though ever nearer fulfilment, never in fact gets beyond a tendency. In like manner, the conclusion in a real or concrete question is foreseen and predicted rather than actually attained; foreseen in the number and direction of accumulated premisses, which all converge to it, and as the result of their combination, approach it more nearly than any assignable difference, yet do not touch it logically (though only not touching it,) on account of the nature of its subject-matter, and the delicate and implicit character of at least part of the reasonings on which it depends. It is by the strength, variety, or multiplicity of premisses, which are only probable, not by invincible syllogisms . . . that the practiced and experienced mind is able to make a sure divination that a conclusion is inevitable, of which his lines of reasoning do not actually put him in possession.[23]

The power of right judgment which recognizes that these converging probabilities are true grounds for certitude is a natural gift, or function of the intellect, which Newman calls the Illative Sense.[24] It is by means of this Illative Sense that the average man can

[23] *Ibid.*, pp. 320 f.
[24] Cf. *ibid.*, p. 342. Father D'Arcy writes: "This Illative Sense is Newman's answer to the problem that he set out to solve. That certainty is a state which all of us can verify he assumes; he has argued also that certitude is not a passive impression made upon the mind, but in all concrete questions an active recognition of propositions as true. Now reason never bids us be certain except on absolute proof, and, nevertheless, formal inference cannot be more than conditional, cannot produce more than the probable. What criterion then can there be which will warrant our certitude? The answer is that the sole and final judgment on the validity of an inference in concrete matter is committed to a mental faculty, the Illative Sense" (*op. cit.*, p. 141).

have a real certitude of the fundamental truths of religion without depending on the traditional logically
demonstrative proofs.

The next section of the *Grammar* is devoted to an
analysis of the sanction, the nature, and the range of
this Illative Sense, illustrated with a wealth of example.
Newman insists on the naturalness of the Illative Sense.
In concrete conclusions, he affirms, "there is no
ultimate test of truth besides the testimony born to
truth by the mind itself, and . . . this phenomenon,
perplexing as we may find it, is a normal and inevitable
characteristic of the mental constitution of a being like
man on a stage such as the world." [25] It is enough for
the proof of the value and authority of any function
which a man possesses, Newman maintains, to be able
to pronounce that it is natural.[26] He explains the nature
of the Illative Sense by drawing a parallel with good
judgment, or prudence, in conduct—what Aristotle
calls *phronesis*. Although truth is ever one and the
same, and certitude is immutable, "still the reasonings
which carry us on to truth and certitude are many and
distinct, and vary with the inquirer," so that there is
a real and necessary place for a controlling principle
(the Illative Sense) in inferences preceding certitude.[27] Newman next points out the vast range of the

[25] *G.A.*, p. 350.
[26] Cf. *ibid.*, p. 347.
[27] Cf. *ibid.*, pp. 353–56.

Illative Sense—every subject matter of thought.[28] His theory is thus complete.

In the last chapters, Newman applies this theory to belief in revealed religion. This positive apologetic will strike many readers as the weakest part of the *Grammar*. But this is not surprising when we consider that Newman was not professing his apologetic to be *the* proof of Christianity, but merely that evidence from the convergence of probabilities which was personally convincing to him.[29] He does not maintain that everyone will be convinced by it, though he naturally hopes and expects that many will be.

[28] Cf. *ibid.*, p. 360–83.
[29] Cf. *ibid.*, p. 385.

CHAPTER XVII

THE PRINCIPAL CRITICISM: DOES THE *GRAMMAR* UNDERMINE THE FOUNDATIONS OF OBJECTIVE RELIGIOUS TRUTH?

IN A LETTER dated March 2, 1870, John Henry Newman, with what seems an undercurrent of amused and slightly weary resignation, wrote: "You will be disappointed with my 'Grammar,' and so will everyone be. It is what it is, and it is not what it is not; and what it is not most people will expect that it is." [1] These lines, written before the *Grammar of Assent* had issued from the publisher's, were singularly prophetic.

We do not mean to say, of course, that everyone has been disappointed in the *Grammar*. Quite to the contrary, it has been hailed as a masterpiece of intuitive psychology by such penetrating philosophers and critics as Michael Maher, S.J., and, in recent years, by M. C. D'Arcy, S.J. [2] But many of the critics of New-

[1] *Letters and Correspondence of John Henry Newman,* edited by Anne Mozley (London: Longmans, Green and Co., 1890), II, 429.

[2] Father Maher remarks the "rare skill" and the "clearness and felicitous richness" with which Newman illustrated the field of our actual

man have singled out the *Grammar of Assent* for their special attention, and quite a number of them seem to be under the impression that (to borrow Newman's phrase) it is what it is not.

Since in this study we are interested in Newman's theological thought, we shall confine our examination of the criticisms of the *Grammar* to those which are directed, not necessarily by theologians, but from a theological viewpoint. We do not believe that we are guilty of a synthetic oversimplification when we maintain that the charges that the *Grammar of Assent* is theologically pernicious are almost all founded in a disregard of what we have indicated as the second principle to be observed in a critical perusal of Newman's works: that they must be judged in accordance with the precise purpose for which they were written and the characteristics of the readers for whom they were intended.

As a type of this sort of criticism, Charles Sarolea has given us a convenient formula, which is, we suppose, part of his considerable contribution to the "ingenious misunderstanding" of Newman which he recommended: "*The Grammar of Assent* was only a Catholic version of the *Analogy* of Butler, and might be

---

rational life (cf. *Psychology: Empirical and Rational*, 6th ed., London: Longmans, Green and Co., 1908, p. 324). Father D'Arcy observes that "much has been written on this subject since his [Newman's] day, but the *Grammar of Assent* still remains the masterpiece which no one can safely neglect" (*op. cit.*, p. 107).

interpreted and held as undermining the foundations of absolute and objective religious truth." [3]

It is also, we believe, to a misunderstanding of the scope of the theory contained in the *Grammar* (and tentatively in the *University Sermons*) that many impressions of Newman as "antirational" may be traced, since in these volumes is contained a Newman theory of belief which, on superficial examination, seems to underrate the value and importance of formal logic as a source of certitude. There seems to be no other basis for positions such as that of Henri Brémond, who maintained that Newman, although gifted with a lucid, ingenious, and subtle intelligence, took pleasure in abasing reason; and that if he were not of a singularly robust faith, he would be the most formidable of the professors of skepticism. [4]

The examination, then, of the charge that the theory of belief set forth by Newman in the *Grammar of Assent* destroys the foundations of objective certitude has a distinct importance in the correction of the too frequent popular picture of Newman as an intellectual

[3] *Op. cit.*, p. 83. To this criticism may be reduced such agnostic interpretations of the *Grammar* as that of Leslie Stephen: "What Newman offers as a logical process is really an analysis of the conditions of conviction, which proves that one condition is illogical, and he therefore, so far, destroys the authority of the conviction. He has clearly shown why people entertain a belief in the absence of any reason for maintaining it" (*An Agnostic's Apology* [London: Smith, Elder and Co., 1893], p. 229).

[4] Cf. *Newman.—Essai de biographie psychologique* (Paris: Bloud et Cie., 1913), p. 18.

saved from skepticism only by his unwavering faith.

Can the *Grammar of Assent* be regarded as "undermining the foundations of absolute and objective religious truth"? Only on the hypothesis that it is what it is not and was not intended to be. If Newman wrote the *Grammar* as his version of the only method of proving the objective truth of Christianity; if he wrote it to show the objective inadequacy of the scientific proofs for God's existence; if he wrote it to prove that the traditional theological treatises on the evidences of Christianity are useless; if he outlined his theory as the one valid basis for certitude in matters of religion: then the critics whose opinions are similar to that of Dr. Sarolea would be very close to the truth.

But Newman did none of these things. The *Grammar of Assent* has only one intention: to prove that the average man, ignorant of the scientific proofs for God's existence and unacquainted with the traditional apologetics of the Schools, does arrive at a real certitude of the truth of Christianity. Far from undermining the objective certitude (or, as Newman would say, the certainty) of the truth of revealed religion, Newman wrote the *Grammar* merely to show that the certitude which the common man has of that truth is a valid certitude; that his faith is a true and rational faith, in spite of his lack of knowledge of scientific proofs. Newman does not deny the traditional proofs for the existence of God, nor does he depreciate scientific apologetics; he simply maintains that the faith of a man unversed in these matters is both certain and valid. Of course Newman does not impugn the supernatural character of faith; he deals with the *rationality* of faith, with what we might call its natural preamble.

There are, then, two points to be illustrated: first, that Newman, in writing the *Grammar*, really had in mind the purpose we have attributed to him; and secondly, that Newman, in pursuit of that aim, did not deny the validity of traditional, objective, scientific proofs.

With regard to the first point, we must realize that the *Grammar* was Newman's final exposition of a problem that had been tentatively treated in the *Oxford University Sermons* and that had occupied his mind, off and on, for the greater part of his life: the problem of why the average man believes.[5] In 1860, Newman wrote to Dr. Meynell, professor of philosophy at Oscott, who had expressed his appreciation of the *University Sermons:*

I have had some correspondence with a dear old Protestant friend, who wished me to write a book, on what would really be the same subject expanded—so now I am more inclined to do something or other on the subject, but less certain whether or not to re-issue the Sermons. If I wrote a new work, it would be on "the popular, practical, and personal evidence of Christianity"—i.e. as contrasted to the scientific, and its object would be to show that a given

5 Cf. Wilfrid Ward, *op. cit.,* II, 242 f.

individual, high or low, has as much right (has as real rational grounds) to be certain, as a learned theologian who knows the scientific evidence.[6]

The "new work" with the purpose indicated was not published for ten more years. It was the *Grammar of Assent*.

Throughout the course of the *Grammar* itself, Newman's purpose is kept continually before the reader. In the chapter concluding the first part, for instance, Newman applies what he has been saying of apprehension and assent to the matter of religion. His intention is to consider the dogmas of the Being of God and of the Divine Trinity in Unity, in their relation to assent, and he warns the reader: "I am not proposing to set forth the arguments which issue in the belief of these doctrines, but to investigate what it is to believe in them, what the mind does, what it contemplates, when it makes an act of faith." [7] Thus it is not Newman's aim to propose the objective criteria which are sufficient for the proof of Christianity. That the average man can, in his own mind, be fully convinced of the truth of Christianity, Newman accepts as a fact of experience. He is interested in the rational validity of that conviction.

A letter highly important for the light it throws on the theory which ultimately developed into the *Gram-*

[6] *Ibid.*, p. 243.
[7] *G.A.*, p. 99.

mar of Assent was written by Newman to William Froude, brother of Hurrell, in 1860. It illustrates the high regard in which Newman held the certitude of the ordinary man in matters of faith. The letter reads in part:

Speaking under the correction of my fuller thought I should say

(1) that I not only do not mean that there is anything sophistical in the principles on which non-religious truth is pursued at present, but that theologians, (who ought to know in Arte sua) all affirm that Christianity is proved by the same rigorous scientific processes by which it is proved that we have an Indian Empire or that the earth goes around the sun. . . .

(2) But the scientific proof of Christianity is not the popular, practical, personal evidence on which a given individual believes in it. . . . I should differ from you, if I understand you, in thinking that there is a popular and personal way of arriving at certainty in Christianity as logical as that which is arrived at by scientific methods in subjects non-religious. . . .

I consider the proof (grounds) on which a given individual believes in Christianity . . . lead legitimately not only to opinion or passive acceptance but to certainty as cogent as scientific proof. Nay I go further, I think that [there] is a sophism in (considering) the certainty of secular science so far superior to the certainty, or persuasion as you would call it, of the personal evidence for Christianity.[8]

[8] Gordon Huntington Harper, *Cardinal Newman and William Froude, F.R.S., a Correspondence* (Baltimore: The Johns Hopkins Press, 1933), pp. 131 f. The letters, hitherto largely unpublished, contained in this collection, are of the utmost value to the student of the *Grammar of Assent*. To mention only one feature, they show how Newman was influenced in the choice of argument for his *Grammar*

Newman's 1860 opinion had not changed in 1870. The *Grammar of Assent* made no pretense of being a manual of apologetics. It was concerned, not with the scientific proof of Christianity, but with the "popular, practical, personal evidence on which a given individual believes in it."

Sylvester Juergens has capably summarized the differences between Newman's aim in the *Grammar* and that of the traditional apologist:

> Newman's purpose, it must be recalled, in studying the origin and evolution of the process that leads up to the real assent called divine faith, is not to prove that human reason can be certain that a given revelation is divine, but to show how an ordinary Christian is certain that Christianity is divine. He does not attempt a theoretical defence of the possibility of a rational assent which may be given to the certainty that Christianity is a message from God. That is the aim of the Science of the Evidences of Religion called Apologetics. . . . Newman's aim, however, is to describe in broad outlines the complex, implicit, psychological process as it unfolds, gradually in the honest pagan who follows the light of conscience, or instantaneously, intuitively, in the Christian by birth when he comes to the use of reason, by which process both of these men are led to accept and hold firmly the divinity of the Gospel. Newman attempts to show not only how ordinary men come to believe but also why they are justified in their assent.

---

by the concession on the part of the scientist and freethinker Froude of the possibility of "spiritual insight" which would enable a man to see beyond the measure of ordinary men. We might remark that, while the correspondence itself and much of the commentary are highly illuminating, a few of the editor's conclusions are not, in our opinion, to be accepted unreservedly.

His aim differs from that of the traditional school of apologists in this that, while the latter demonstrates that human reason has irrefragable proofs for its certitude in the divinity of Christianity, his sole object is to show that the average man has a proof sufficient for his own needs, though he ordinarily cannot analyze this proof, give it proper expression and skillfully defend it against attack. The former is a theoretical defence of human reason's right of assenting to the Gospel, the latter is a practical illustration of how any man who is aided by grace comes to certain faith by following the laws of his nature.[9]

It seems, then, to be unquestionably true that (in the words of Wilfrid Ward) "the one avowed object of the 'Essay on Assent' was to show that simple and uneducated minds could have rational grounds for belief in Christianity without knowledge of its scientific evidences." [10] So much for our first point.

Secondly, although Newman was treating the subject of belief from a subjective, psychological point of view, he did not deny the objective validity of the traditional proofs. He recognized that the great, fundamental truths of religion "may be proved and defended by an array of invincible logical arguments," and he refused to admit the notion that religion has not "irrefragable arguments" in its behalf.[11] As to the existence of God, Newman formally subscribes to the conventional objective proofs and their complete de-

[9] *Op. cit.*, pp. 148 f.
[10] *Op. cit.*, II, 246.
[11] Cf. *G.A.*, p. 336.

monstrative value, even while he admits that of all arguments the one which is brought home most strongly and vividly to him is that from conscience.[12]

The absence from the *Grammar of Assent* of any exposition of the traditional proofs for the existence of God has been severely criticized by Father Léonce de Grandmaison, who calls their omission an "enormous defect." [13] But should we not rather be surprised if they were to be found there? Newman's purpose (we repeat at the risk of becoming tedious) is not to present the objective proofs of the fundamental truths of religion, but to prove the validity of the certitude of the average, simple, ordinary, unscientific human being in matters of faith.

If we consider also (still in the light of our second principle of criticism) for whom the *Grammar* was intended, the case for the omission is even clearer. Newman, himself an Englishman, was writing for Englishmen, whose mental processes and predilections he so well understood. The proofs for the existence of God, though absolutely probative, are not easy to grasp, and require a certain metaphysical culture. Newman's conception of the English character, founded on his own consciousness of it, was that it found metaphysics uncongenial. Was it unusual that he should eschew metaphysical proofs, however pow-

---

[12] Cf. *ibid.*, p. 500.
[13] Cf. article "John Henry Newman considéré comme maître," *Etudes,* CX (1907), 43 f.

erful, and stress a method which he felt to be in entire accord with the English mentality? He was not writing a theological textbook; he was describing and analyzing the testimony of his own consciousness in the hope that he could help others similarly constituted.[14]

We may briefly summarize the general argument of this chapter thus: it is difficult to see how the *Grammar of Assent*, treating as it does only of the certitude of the ordinary man, and careful, moreover, to maintain the unquestionable probative value of the objective, traditional proofs for the fundamental verities of religion, can be regarded as undermining the objectivity of religious truth; unless, of course, we were to examine the *Grammar* with no thought at all of the purpose for which it was written or of those for whom it was intended.

[14] It is interesting to note that what is perhaps Newman's best testimony to the efficacy and necessity of the conventional proofs is to be found in the one volume of his works which is composed largely of discourses not delivered in England. The passage (*Idea*, pp. 25, 28 f.) is part of an address delivered in Ireland.

CHAPTER XVIII

THE *GRAMMAR OF ASSENT* AND THE MODERNISTS

ON JULY 3, 1907, the Sacred Congregation of the Holy Office issued a decree beginning with the words *Lamentabili sane exitu,* and listing and condemning sixty-five propositions of the Modernists. The twenty-fifth proposition to be proscribed read: "The assent of faith is ultimately founded on a collection of probabilities." [1] "This," wrote Alfred Loisy flatly, "was Newman's doctrine." Loisy "did not wish to believe that the Sacred Congregation desired to condemn Newman," so he advanced the theory that the proposition might have been found in the works of some of Newman's "disciples" or in Houtin's writings or in a late work of his own. The impression he undoubtedly wishes to convey is that the Congregation, by condemning the Modernists for holding such a doctrine, had, whether it wished to or not, condemned Newman with them. [2]

[1] "Assensus fidei ultimo innititur in congerie probabilitatum." *A.S.S.,* XL (1907), 473.
[2] "XXV. *The assent of faith rests ultimately on an accumulation of probabilities.* This was Newman's doctrine. I reproduced it in an article

The first question to be considered in this chapter is whether Newman's theory of probabilities as definitively outlined in the *Grammar of Assent* was of such a nature as to fall under the condemnation expressed in proposition twenty-five.

It will be remarked that the proposition speaks only of a collection ("congeries") of probabilities. It does not speak of the convergence of probabilities, and we have indeed no right to stretch the condemnation to include this method of proof by convergence, a method which, so far as we know, no authoritative Catholic apologist has repudiated.[3]

---

on the proofs and the economy of revelation, which I published in the *Revue du clergé français* of March 15, 1900. I doubt that the Sacred Congregation has gone back as far as this article. I doubt still more that the Congregation intended to condemn Newman. On the other hand, I do not find this proposition in my writings of the last few years. Either the Sacred Congregation has taken it from some disciple of Newman, or simply garnered it from the *Question biblique au XXe siècle* of M. Houtin, where my article is quoted (p. 75); or else it turned into a general proposition the words: 'rational probabilities of this article of faith,' which I used with regard to the divinity of Christ (*Autour d'un petit livre*, p. 129)." *Simples réflexions . . .*, pp. 64 f. In late years Loisy renewed the charge (cf. *Mémoires . . .*, II, 548).

[3] There is no need of supposing (as some have done) that this twenty-fifth proposition of the decree *Lamentabili* represents Newman's theory concerning the proof of the fact of revelation by 'convergence of probabilities.' Is it in any degree likely, moreover, that Cardinal Newman, and for a very defensible theory . . . should have been numbered among the partisans of this 'synthesis of all heresies,' as Pius X characterized Modernism?" (S. Harent, article "Foi," *D.T.C.*, Vol. VI, col. 195).

The method of proof from convergent probabilities has been clearly set forth by H. Pinard de la Boullaye, S.J., in *L'étude comparée des religions* (Paris: Beauchesne, 1925), II, 388–424; and by A. Gardeil, O.P., in *La crédibilité et l'apologétique* (Paris: Gabalda et Cie., 1912), pp. 161–201. A brief, "popular" treatment of the same subject may

A sufficient number of independent facts, each in itself only a probable indication, but all converging toward one explanation, one justifying reason, one solution, are a legitimate source of certitude. Why? Because there must be a reason for this convergence, and the proof is thus based, not on the fact that our multiple indications are only probable, but that their convergence toward one solution must have a reason, and that the reason can be only the truth of that solution toward which the probabilities point. Thus the probabilities coalesce to form a certain, factual premise of an implicit syllogism, the other premise being the certain principle of sufficient reason, and the conclusion thus being certain.

Newman's method of proof from probabilities was, in effect, nothing more nor less than this. He did not maintain that certitude was based on the mere collection of probabilities, but in their unanimous convergence toward one, and only one, solution or explanation.[4]

---

be found in a fairly recent volume of apologetics by Joseph Falcon, S.M. (*La crédibilité du dogme catholique* [Paris: Emmanuel Vitte, 1933], pp. 113–15.) S. Harent in the article "Foi" which we have cited above, also gives an excellent outline of this method of proof. (D.T.C., Vol. VI, cols. 195–98.)

[4] Cf., for example, *G.A.*, pp. 320 f. (quoted in chap. 16 above); and *G.A.*, pp. 319 f. (quoted below). S. Harent writes: "Newman ne parle que de probabilités 'convergentes'; la proposition 25 ne reproduit pas ce mot, capital dans sa théorie" (Harent, *loc. cit.*).

It is worth noting also that Newman attached a precise meaning to the word "probability." By a "probability" he meant a fact, not necessarily of doubtful probative value, but merely *not demonstrative* (cf. above, chap. 13, A).

Newman also (and this is a point which seems to have escaped the notice of those authors who have defended him against Loisy's charge) clearly implies the use of the principle of sufficient reason, although naturally he brought nothing so "metaphysical" explicitly into the *Grammar*. Discussing the proof of revelation, he wrote:

Here, as in Astronomy, is the same absence of demonstration of the thesis, the same cumulating and converging indications of it, the same indirectness in the proof, as being *per impossibile*, the same recognition nevertheless that the conclusion is not only probable but true.[5]

The logical form of this argument, is, as I have already observed, indirect, viz. that "the conclusion cannot be otherwise," and Butler says that an event is proved, if its antecedents "could not in reason be supposed to have happened *unless* it were true," and law-books tell us that the principle of circumstantial evidence is the *reductio ad absurdum*.[6]

The proof by converging probabilities is "indirect," "*per impossibile*," etc., simply because there must be a sufficient reason for the convergence; because such a convergence would be impossible without this reason; and because the conclusion to which the probabilities tend cannot be otherwise than as indicated by these probabilities, because there would then be no sufficient reason for their convergence upon it.

Without saying so in the exact words, Newman has thus shown that his theory clearly implies, as an in-

[5] *G.A.,* pp. 319 f.
[6] *Ibid.,* pp. 321 f.

tegral part, the principle of sufficient reason. If the Illative Sense, as Newman holds, recognizes the certitude which is the valid result of this convergence of probabilities, we may attribute the fact to its quasi-instinctive recognition of the principle of sufficient reason as a law of being and of thought.

Evidently anyone who takes a little trouble to ascertain Newman's exact meaning and to view his theory as a whole, and then to compare it with the error condemned in the decree *Lamentabili*, would hardly fall into the mistake of gratuitously extending the condemnation of the Holy See to one whom it has never intended to encompass.

The second question for consideration in this chapter is whether the Modernists faithfully reproduced Newman's doctrine. Essentially the question is already answered by the facts: had they done so, their theory about probabilities would not have been condemned. As Christian Pesch, S.J., remarks, if the Modernists had been content with maintaining, as did Newman, simply that moral certitude is often arrived at by arguments which, taken one by one, are only probable and that this is a sufficient certitude for the preambles of faith, they would have held nothing but the truth.[7]

To bring our discussion down to concrete details,

[7] Cf. *Praelectiones dogmaticae* (Freiburg: Herder, 3d ed., 1910), VIII, 131 f.

we will let Alfred Loisy be the spokesman for the Modernist "disciples" of Newman. In maintaining that Newman was included in the condemnation contained in proposition XXV of *Lamentabili*, Loisy claimed to have "reproduced" Newman's doctrine in his article of March 15, 1900, in the *Revue du clergé français*. He also suggested that the Sacred Congregation may have found their censurable proposition in a volume of Houtin's which cited this article. We are, then, within our rights in using this Loisy article as an example of the way the Modernists understood and "reproduced" Newman's theory.[8]

On reading the article, we are struck by a surprising circumstance. Instead of citing the work in which Newman treats his doctrine *ex professo* and in detail— the *Grammar of Assent*—the only quotation from the Cardinal which Loisy uses in the course of the entire article is a passage from the *Apologia pro Vita Sua*. The context in which Loisy places this citation is remarkable:

True religion is made to be known, experienced, lived, and this intimate experience has always been its true demonstration, changeable in its logical expression according to time and even persons, certain for all who believe, that is, for

[8] Cf. *supra*, note 2 to this chapter. For a general analysis of the Modernist position regarding the assent of faith and the argument from probabilities, and a comparison, along very broad lines, with Newman's theory, the reader may consult S. Harent, "Foi," *D.T.C.*, Vol. VI, cols. 194 f.

those who, regarding religion closely enough to know it well in itself and in relation to themselves, have the courage to embrace it by an act of the will. . . . The most learned demonstration changes nothing regarding these conditions essential to faith. Here is what Cardinal Newman has written: "I say, that I believed in God on a ground of probability, that I believed in Christianity on a probability, and that I believed in Catholicism on a probability, and that these three grounds of probability, distinct from each other of course in subject matter, were still all of them one and the same in nature of proof, as being probabilities—probabilities of a special kind, a cumulative, a transcendent probability but still probability; inasmuch as He who made us has so willed, that in mathematics indeed we should arrive at certitude by rigid demonstration, but in religious inquiry we should arrive at certitude by accumulated probabilities;— He has willed, I say, that we should so act, and, as willing it, He co-operates with us in our acting, and thereby enables us to do that which He wills us to do, and carries us on, if our will does but co-operate with His, to a certitude which rises higher than the logical force of our conclusions." In other words, the demonstration is perfected in the very reality of faith, in its substantial truth, from whence glows upon the mass of probabilities the ray of light which illumines them, the life which animates them, and the unshakable certitude which binds them together. Faith, we repeat, does not cease to be profoundly reasonable, although it is not an affair of rational speculation; but its high rationability appears in its full evidence only to those who sincerely desire to know it, and who are not afraid of the truth. There is nothing to prevent the ignorant man from succeeding after his fashion just as well as the learned, without so much research and discussion.

This understood, the certitude of revelation is not diminished; it is referred to its true character, which is to be a certitude of faith, and not a scientific certitude.[9]

Here, as in most of Alfred Loisy's writings before his final break with the Church, we find a strange mixture of verbal orthodoxy side by side with the dangerously tendentious, and between the lines the suggestion of a mode of thought completely untenable for a Catholic.

Loisy involves in a hopeless confusion the absolute supernatural certitude which is the concomitant result of the divinely infused virtue of faith and the natural moral certitude which can be evoked by the spectacle of the multitude of probable arguments all converging

[9] "La vraie religion est faite pour être connue, expérimentée, vécue, et cette expérience intime en a toujours été la véritable démonstration, variable dans son expression logique selon les temps et même les personnes, certaine pour tous ceux qui croient, c'est à dire qui, voyant d'assez près la religion pour la bien connaître en elle-même et par rapport à eux, ont le courage d'y adhérer volontairement. . . . La démonstration la plus savante ne change rien à ces conditions essentielles de la foi. Voici ce qu'en écrit le cardinal Newman: [Here Loisy gives the French translation of the text from pages 199–200 of the *Apologia* which we have repeated above]. En d'autres termes, la démonstration s'achève dans la réalité même de la foi, dans sa vérité substantielle, d'où rejaillit sur la masse des probabilités le rayon qui les éclaire, la vie qui les anime et la certitude inébranlable qui les rassemble. La foi, disons-le encore, ne laisse pas d'être profondément raisonnable, bien qu'elle ne soit pas affaire de spéculation rationnelle; mais sa haute raison n'apparaît en toute évidence qu'à ceux qui veulent sincèrement la connaître et qui n'ont pas peur de la vérité. Rien n'empêche les ignorants d'y réussir à leur manière aussi bien que les savants, sans tant de recherches et de discussions.

Pour être ainsi comprise, la certitude de la révélation n'est pas diminuée; elle est ramenée à son véritable caractère, qui est d'être une certitude de foi et non une certitude scientifique" (*Revue du clergé français*, Vol. XXII, no. 128 [March 15, 1900], pp. 142 f.).

toward the proof of revelation. It is his theory that only faith gives to the probabilities their probative value in the first place; it is only after faith has come, and in its light, that he would have the believer realize the cogent power of the convergent mass of probable arguments. He follows his quotation from Newman with the sentence: "In other words, the demonstration is perfected in the very reality of faith, in its substantial truth, from whence glows upon the mass of probabilities the ray of light which illumines them, and the unshakable certitude which binds them together." But this is not at all Newman's meaning "in other words." To affirm, as Loisy does, that it is faith which recognizes the argument from probabilities as the basis of certitude, is an illegitimate extension of Newman's statement, which speaks merely of God's cooperation with a well-intentioned inquirer in the examination of the multiple probable arguments, prior to faith. For Newman, the convergence of probabilities in itself, logically preceding faith, forms a sufficient argument for the rational certitude of that faith.

So even Newman's words as they stand are a far cry from the inference Loisy draws from them. But Loisy has torn Newman's statement from its context and inserted it in an altogether alien one. In this passage Newman had no intention of establishing the theory of the argument from convergent probabilities. He realized perfectly that his words were neither a theo-

logically exact nor a theoretically precise statement of
the argument. This is clear from the explanation which
he prefaced to the passage in the *Apologia*, and which
Loisy neglected to include in his quotation. "Let it be
recollected," Newman warned, "that I am historically
relating my state of mind, at the period of my life
which I am surveying. I am not speaking theologically,
nor have I any intention of going into controversy, or
of defending myself; but speaking historically of what
I held in 1843-4, I say . . ." (Then follow the words
cited by Loisy.) [10] This passage, therefore, is merely
Newman's historical relation of the state of his mind
as an Anglican, of what he held and believed in the last
years preceding his entrance into the Catholic Church.
To call such a citation the "reproduction" of Newman's "doctrine" on the manner in which the assent of
faith may be considered to depend on probabilities is
not the act of a sincere "disciple."

In addition to grafting on to Newman's words a
meaning quite alien, Loisy has thus misrepresented the
Cardinal because he has violated the elementary rule
against tearing statements from their context (which
forbids a fortiori their use in a context totally different) and because he has failed, unwittingly or deliberately, to observe the second principle which we have
been speaking of: that to understand the scope and
significance of a passage from Newman we must keep

[10] *Apo.*, p. 199.

in mind Newman's purpose in writing those particular lines.

It might be objected that M. Loisy, in stating that he had "reproduced" Newman's doctrine, did not mean that he had cited it directly, but that, in the course of his article, he had expressed it in his own words. A reading of the article in the *Revue du clergé français* is sufficient to refute this objection. Loisy's theory, as expressed in his own words, was far distant from Newman's, and entirely discordant with the final expression of Newman's thought on the subject in the *Grammar of Assent*. As we do not wish to prolong this chapter unduly, we will let a significant sentence from Loisy's article illustrate this essential discrepancy. We have seen the stress which Newman laid on the *convergence* of probabilities, which the intellect recognizes as an adequate foundation for certitude. But Loisy wrote:

The possessor of the keenest mind, after having studied the bulkiest volumes of apologetics, can remain very undecided and perplexed, if he has consulted only his reason in its function of reasoning, and has limited himself to a critical examination of proofs, inasmuch as each particular proof leads only to a probable conclusion, which does not absolutely exclude the possibility of the opposing conclusion, and the decisive efficacy of the proofs does not depend entirely on their accumulation, which creates for the reason only an extreme probability, but on the intimate experience which is had of it, and on the vital relationship which is established between the searching soul and the truth which presents itself.[11]

Here is the key to the question. Loisy did not believe that probabilities, however cumulative, could lead to certitude, but only to an "extreme probability" which, however "extreme," is still probability. And for him the efficacy of the proof does not lie in convergence, but in "intimate experience," "vital relationship," and so on.

It is not difficult to understand why, in the light of his unorthodox, subjectivist theory, the Modernist Alfred Loisy was condemned by the twenty-fifth proposition of *Lamentabili;* nor is it difficult to understand why Cardinal Newman was not.

11 "Mais l'esprit le plus clairvoyant, après avoir étudié les plus gros livres d'apologétique, peut être encore fort indécis et perplexe, s'il n'a consulté que sa raison raisonnante, et s'il a borné son examen à la critique des preuves, attendu que chaque preuve particulière n'aboutit qu'à une conclusion probable, laquelle n'exclut pas absolument la possibilité de la conclusion opposée, et que l'efficacité décisive des preuves ne dépend pas non plus tout à fait de leur accumulation, qui ne crée encore pour la raison qu'une extrême probabilité, mais de l'experience intime qui en est faite et du rapport vital qui s'établit entre l'âme qui cherche et la vérité qui s'offre" (*Revue du clergé français,* Vol. XXII, no. 128 [March 15, 1900], pp. 140 f.). The "certitude" resulting from this "intimate experience" and "vital relationship" seems to be what Loisy had in mind when he wrote, some years later, of the "moral certitude" justified by the "*ensemble*" of probabilities (cf. *Simples réflexions* . . . p. 70).

CHAPTER XIX

THE POSITIVE VALUE OF THE *GRAMMAR OF ASSENT*

IN SHOWING that the *Grammar of Assent* does not impugn the objective truth of religion, and that its method of proof was not condemned by the decree *Lamentabili*, we have considered the principal theological difficulties against this last major work of John Henry Newman. We believe, however, that something should be said about its positive theological value.

A discussion of this question is necessary mainly because certain features of the philosophy underlying the *Grammar* are open to serious criticism. Any detailed consideration of Newman's philosophy would, of course, be material for another study; but on account of the close relationship of a writer's philosophical principles and his theological thought, we shall examine very briefly the repercussions of one aspect of Newman's philosophy on the positive theological value of the *Grammar of Assent*.

Immediately the old difficulty confronts us again.

Newman's terminology is difficult, not only for the layman, but also (perhaps especially) for one accustomed to the conventions of the Schools. "Anyone coming to the *Grammar* with the intention of fitting the Englishman's notions and divisions into a Schoolman's terminology and method," writes Sylvester Juergens, "will become hopelessly confused, and will inevitably lay it down with the judgment that it is obscurely conceived, recklessly composed, difficult to follow and impossible to understand." [1] We have already considered the particular meanings which Newman gave to "conditional proposition" and "probabilities." His use of the term "Illative Sense" is another example. To adopt the word "sense" in Newman's expression according to the Scholastic usage, which strictly opposes "sense" to "intellect" (as in "nihil in intellectu nisi prius in sensu"), is to misunderstand completely a vital feature of the *Grammar*. With Newman, the Illative Sense was an *intellectual function*, or at least it included purely intellectual operations in its extension: "I have already said that the sole and final judgment on the validity of an inference in concrete matter is committed to the personal action of the ratiocinative faculty, the perfection or virtue of which I have called the Illative Sense, a use of the word 'sense' parallel to our use of it in 'good sense,' 'common sense,' a 'sense of beauty,' &c.;—and I own that I do

[1] *Op. cit.*, p. 18.

not see any way to go farther than this in answer to the question." [2]

Regarding the use of this term, Thomas J. Gerrard has written a careful study; its principal aim is to show that a correct understanding of the term will bring out the fundamental agreement of Newman and St. Thomas Aquinas as opposed to Henri Bergson. Although we cannot agree with the author that there is "perfect harmony" between St. Thomas and Newman, we do most certainly believe that Newman's theory of knowledge is more closely allied to that of St. Thomas than to Bergson's. [3]

The consideration of the meaning given by Newman to such terms as "sense" in "Illative Sense" leads us to a remark that may seem paradoxical: the more we realize the difference in terminology between Newman and the Scholastics, the less is the difference in meaning. Hence the importance again of our third principle of interpretation, which reminds us to take Newman's writing "on its own terms."

However, we hope we have not created the impres-

[2] G.A., p. 345.
[3] Cf. "Bergson, Newman and Aquinas" in The Catholic World, XCVI (March, 1913), 748 ff. In this article the author points out that Bergson conceives of intellectual knowledge as in opposition to, and as being a falsification of sense perception, while St. Thomas and Newman maintain that intellectual perception, receiving its material from sense perception, is the perfection of that lower cognition and not its arbitrary perversion. Our main objection to this essay is its neglect to consider the question of the validity of the universal idea, concerning which it is difficult, to say the least, to reconcile Newman and the great Scholastics.

sion that as soon as we understand the meaning of Newman's terms, all differences between Newman's philosophy and that of the Schools immediately vanish. This would be foreign to our intention and contrary to the truth.

For our part we cannot imagine how any student of philosophy whose training has been along Scholastic lines could fail to acknowledge a grave error in the philosophical structure of the *Grammar of Assent*. In certain critical passages Newman seriously weakens the objective foundation of the universal idea. Instead of being a concept of the essence of a thing, as the Scholastics insist, the universal for Newman was a vague general notion with no applicative value, or at best with an extremely inadequate one, to the knowledge of the individual thing:

> Universals are ever at war with each other; because what is called a universal is only a general; because what is only general does not lead to a necessary conclusion. . . . Let units come first, and (so-called) universals second; let universals minister to units, not units be sacrificed to universals. . . . General laws are not inviolable truths; much less are they necessary causes. Since, as a rule, men are rational, progressive, and social, there is a high probability of this rule being true in the case of a particular person; but we must know him to be sure of it.[4]

In this passage Newman is speaking *ex professo*, and not merely incidentally, of the universal idea, and we

[4] *G.A.*, pp. 279 f.

feel constrained to agree with Father De Grandmaison
that his treatment is purely conceptualist.[5] Newman's
theory of universals is also criticized by Father
D'Arcy, who finds fault with his "habitual disparagement of the notional as compared with the real":

> It looks as if this came from the philosophy he knew best,
> the views of Locke and Hume and Butler. Many of their
> assumptions must have been current in the Oxford of his
> time, and they provided him with what is no better than a
> nominalist theory of knowledge. . . . Almost all that causes
> dissatisfaction in the analysis can be traced back to his theory
> of the notion or universal.[6]

What repercussions does Newman's theory of universals, which results in his "habitual disparagement"
(according to Father D'Arcy) of the notional proposition, have upon his theology? It was Newman's
position that theology deals with dogmas considered
as notional propositions. The Modernists, whose theory of knowledge was akin to that of Henri Bergson,
carried their repudiation of "intellectualism" to the
point of denying the real validity of dogmatic formulas. Is Newman, on the strength of his principles, committed to the same error?

It is clear that he is not. Newman, for whom dogma
was a necessary fundament of religion, postulated an

[5] Cf. article "John Henry Newman considéré comme maître" in
Etudes, CX (January, 1907), 58–62.

[6] *Op. cit.*, pp. 148 f. Cf. also Francis Aveling, article "Universals and
the Illative Sense" in *Dublin Review*, CXXXVII (October, 1905),
236 ff.

absolute objective validity for the dogmas of the
Church, even though the propositions expressing these
dogmas may be considered, in theology, as "notional"
in form. Newman taught that a dogma—the same
dogma—could be considered in two ways, as a notional or as a real proposition. He writes, for instance:

> The proposition that there is One Personal and Present
> God may be held in either way; either as a theological truth,
> or as a religious fact or reality. The notion and the reality
> assented-to are represented by one and the same proposition,
> but serve as distinct interpretations of it. When the proposi-
> tion is apprehended for the purposes of proof, analysis, com-
> parison, and the like intellectual exercises, it is used as the
> expression of a notion; when for the purposes of devotion,
> it is the image of a reality. . . . Here we have the solution
> of the common mistake of supposing that there is a con-
> trariety and antagonism between a dogmatic creed and vital
> religion.[7]

Thus, for Newman, the fact that a dogma, considered for the purpose of theological analysis, may be
called "notional," did not in any way detract from its
real significance and objective validity, because it is
not merely notional; it is at the same time real, standing
for a really existing thing. To say, for example, that
"the Blessed Virgin Mary was conceived free from
original sin" is to state a simple fact. We may develop
the idea contained in this proposition into its theological ramifications (i.e., treat it as a notional proposi-

[7] *G.A.*, pp. 119 f.

tion), but the proposition retains an absolute, objective, individual validity just the same. And whether we assent to it as a notional or a real proposition, our assent is unreserved and unconditional. Instead of erecting a barrier between a "dogmatic creed" and a "vital religion," Newman reconciles the two in the same objective foundation of revealed truth. Thus Newman's theory of universals, faulty as it is, does not involve his theology in an anti-intellectualist depreciation of dogmatic formulas.

The *Grammar of Assent* is a definite contribution to theological literature. Newman has performed a valuable service by his insistence on viewing the intellect as a living organism following its own interior laws. The fact which Newman emphasized remains: the average man does not arrive at certitude through logical demonstration, yet his certitude is not therefore invalid. Newman, in stressing faith as a vital act by which the ordinary man, under God's grace, advances to true rational certitude without the aid of "paper logic," has given a worth-while warning to those who cherish the illusion that any given individual may be converted to Catholicism by a polysyllogism.

The basic problem proposed by Newman, and also his method of solution, have a real place in theology. The trained Scholastic will be able to correct the philosophical error of the *Grammar* without fundamentally altering its conclusions.[8] Even for one who does not accept the general theory set forth in Newman's work, the acuteness of its psychological observation, and its carefully selected and vivid illustrations make it an indispensable case-book for the study of the psychology of faith and of conversion.

[8] In *The Nature of Belief*, for example, Father D'Arcy accepts most of Newman's ideas, correcting his notion of universals and substituting for the "Illative Sense" what he prefers to call "interpretation" (cf. *passim*, esp. pp. 147–206).

Conclusion

THE purpose of this study has been to furnish an introduction to Cardinal Newman's theological thought. As the reader has observed, we have attempted neither a complete summary of Newman's teaching nor an examination of all the criticisms of his doctrine. There are many features of his teaching which we have left untouched. Most of these points are theologically irreproachable; a very few—notably his opinion on the inspiration of the *obiter dicta* of Sacred Scripture— leave something to be desired from the standpoint of theological accuracy. But even Homer sometimes nods, and we do not on that account cast reflections on his genius.

Some time ago, when we first began to think upon the subject matter of this study, we decided upon two things: first, that any "preface" to Newman's theology should not be a mere reproduction of the salient points of his teaching (Newman can speak for himself much better than anyone else can speak for him), but a convenient synthesis of the background material necessary for the true interpretation of that teaching. We attempted such a synthesis in the first part of our study, organizing this background material into four "principles." Whether we have to any degree succeeded is for the reader to determine; but our opinion as to the necessity of such a synthesis has not changed. We hope that the work will be taken up by hands more capable than ours.

We also believed that any introduction to Newman's theology should attempt to clear away some of the vague suspicion of Newman's theological thought, a suspicion which is so shadowy and unformulated, but present in many minds. To this end we examined, in the light of the principles of interpretation, what seemed to us the most important criticisms of Newman's two major—and most frequently attacked—contributions to theological literature, the *Essay on Development* and the *Grammar of Assent*. If we have, in a little, helped to show the weakness of the ground on which these criticisms are based, and to expose the falsity of the "forerunner of Modernism" charge, our study has been more than worth the effort of its writing.

John Henry Newman has all English-speaking Catholics in his debt: the layman desirous of spiritual and intellectual sustenance, the theological student wishing to supplement his studies by an acquaintance with the religious insight and original perspective of a great Catholic intellect, the priest seeking inspiration for his sermons,—all these can find a friend and mentor in Cardinal Newman. And the sincere non-Catholic searching for the faith can find no better guide. If we have awakened in the reader the desire to follow Newman in the original and to treasure up for himself the riches the Cardinal can provide for those who make a genuine effort to understand him, and if the principles we have outlined can be of some help in arriving at that understanding, our purpose has been doubly attained.

Bibliography

Bibliography

I. NEWMAN'S WORKS

The works of Newman listed below are all published by Longmans, Green and Company. The date of the definitive edition of each work is printed in italics. The date in parentheses is that of the reprint used in connection with this study. When the edition we have used is other than that of Longmans, we have so indicated within the parentheses.

WORKS ORIGINALLY WRITTEN BY NEWMAN AS AN ANGLICAN

Two Essays on Biblical and Ecclesiastical Miracles, written in 1825 and 1843; *1870* (1890).

Oxford University Sermons, preached 1826–43; *1871* (1918).

Essays Critical and Historical. Vol. I written 1828–40; *1871*. (London: Basil Montagu Pickering, 1871.)

Lectures on Justification, 1838; *1874* (1892).

The Arians of the Fourth Century, 1833; *1871* (1890).

Parochial and Plain Sermons, *1868* (1891).

    Vol. I, preached 1825–33; published 1834.

    Vol. II, preached 1830–35; published 1835.

    Vol. III, preached 1829–35; published 1836.

    Vol. IV, preached 1835–38; published 1839.

    Vol. V, preached 1834–40; published 1840.

    Vol. VI, preached 1836–41; published 1842.

    Vol. VII, preached 1825–42; published 1842–43.

    Vol. VIII, preached 1825–43; published 1842–43.

The Via Media

    Vol. I, 1837; *1877* (1891).

    Vol. II, 1830–45; *1883* (1891).

Sermons on Subjects of the Day, preached 1831–43; published 1843; *1869*. (London: Rivington's, 1879).

Select Treatises on St. Athanasius, 2 vols., 1841–44; *1881* (1890).

An Essay on the Development of Christian Doctrine, 1845, published after Newman's reception into the Catholic Church; *1878* (1890). We cite also the edition published in New York by D. Appleton, 1845.

WORKS ORIGINALLY WRITTEN BY NEWMAN
AS A CATHOLIC

Loss and Gain, the Story of a Convert, *1848* (1903).

Discourses to Mixed Congregations, *1849* (1892).

Difficulties of Anglicans

    Vol. I, *1850* (1891).

Vol. II, 1865–75; *1875* (1891).

Sermons on Various Occasions, preached 1850–73; *1874* (1891).

Present Position of Catholics in England, 1851; *1872* (1889).

The Idea of a University, 1852, 1859; *1873* (1912).

Callista, a Tale of the Third Century, 1856; *1888* (1890).

Apologia pro Vita Sua, first published in seven parts on consecutive Thursdays between April 21 and June 2, 1864, with an Appendix published June 16, 1864. *1865* (1890). We have also used for this study the first American edition (New York: D. Appleton, 1865), which reproduces the 1864 form of the *Apologia*, not Newman's revised edition of 1865.

An Essay in Aid of a Grammar of Assent, 1870; *1885* (1891).

Sermon Notes of John Henry Cardinal Newman 1849–1878, edited by Fathers of the Birmingham Oratory, *1913* (1913).

Addresses to Cardinal Newman with His Replies 1879–1881, edited by Rev. W. P. Neville, *1905* (1905).

Meditations and Devotions of the Late Cardinal Newman (Collected Papers). Introduction by W. P. Neville, *1893* (1893).

(The two principal collections of Newman's letters are listed below among the biographical sources.)

VOLUMES CONTAINING MATERIAL ORIGINALLY WRITTEN DURING BOTH THE ANGLICAN AND CATHOLIC PERIODS OF NEWMAN'S LIFE

Essays Critical and Historical
> Vol. II, written 1840–46; *1871*. (London: Basil Montagu Pickering, 1871.)

Discussions and Arguments, written 1836–66; *1872* (1891).

Historical Sketches, *1873* (1891).
> Vol. I, written 1824–53.
> Vol. II, written 1833–73.
> Vol. III, written 1834–72.

Tracts Theological and Ecclesiastical, written 1835–72; *1874* (1891).

Verses on Various Occasions, written 1818–65; *1868* (1890).

II. BIOGRAPHIES OF NEWMAN AND STUDIES OF HIS THOUGHT

THE MAJOR BIOGRAPHICAL SOURCES

WARD, WILFRID. The Life of John Henry Cardinal Newman. New York: Longmans, 1912. 2 vols.

Letters and Correspondence of John Henry Newman, with a Brief Autobiography, edited by Anne Mozley. London: Longmans, 1890. 2 vols.

Correspondence of John Henry Newman with John Keble and Others, 1839–1845, edited at the Birmingham Oratory. London: Longmans, 1917.

OTHER BIOGRAPHIES AND STUDIES OF NEWMAN

The books listed from this point on are not all of equal value. The fact of inclusion in the bibliography does not mean that a book is recommended for general reading. Those volumes on the *Index of Forbidden Books* are indicated by an asterisk.

AMBRUZZI, ALOYSIUS, S.J. The Newman Book of Religion. London: Coldwell, 1937.

BARRY, WILLIAM. Newman. London: Hodder & Stoughton, 1904. Second edition.

———. "Newman" in The Catholic Encyclopedia. New York: The Universal Knowledge Foundation, 1907–12.

BELLASIS, EDWARD. Coram Cardinali. London: Longmans, 1916.

BELLOC, HILAIRE. Apologia pro Vita Sua, edited for college use by Daniel M. O'Connell, S.J., with a foreword by Hilaire Belloc. Chicago: Loyola University Press, 1930.

BRÉMOND, HENRI. Newman. Le développement du dogme chrétien. Paris: Bloud et Cie., 1906. Fifth edition.

————. Newman. Psychologie de la foi. Paris: Bloud et Cie., 1905. Third edition.

————. Newman. La vie chrétienne. Paris: Bloud et Cie., 1906. Third edition.

————. Newman. Essai de biographie psychologique. Paris: Bloud et Cie., 1913. English version, The Mystery of Newman, translated by H. C. Corrance. Introduction by Rev. George Tyrrell. London: Williams & Norgate, 1907.

BYRNE, JAMES J. "The Notion of Doctrinal Development in the Anglican Writings of J. H. Newman" in Sylloge excerptorum e dissertationibus ad gradum Doctoris in Sacra Theologia vel in Iure canonico consequendum conscriptis, tomus IV, Annus academicus 1935–1936 (Lovanii: Sumptibus Bibliothecae Universitatis, 1937).

D'CRUZ, F. A. Cardinal Newman, His Place in Religion and in Literature. Madras, India: The Good Pastor Press. Undated.

ELBERT, JOHN A., S.M. Evolution of Newman's Conception of Faith. Philadelphia: The Dolphin Press, 1932.

FOLGHERA, J. D., O.P. Newman Apologiste. Paris: Editions de la Revue des Jeunes, 1927. English version, Newman's Apologetic, by Philip Hereford, with an introduction by Bede Jarrett, O.P. London: Sands & Co., 1928.

FRIEDEL, FRANCIS J., S.M. The Mariology of Cardinal Newman. New York: Benziger Bros., 1928.

GUITTON, JEAN. La Philosophie de Newman. Paris: Boivin et Cie., 1933.

HARPER, GORDON HUNTINGTON. Cardinal Newman and William Froude F.R.S., a Correspondence. Baltimore: The Johns Hopkins Press, 1933.

HARROLD, CHARLES F. A Newman Treasury, Selections from the Prose Works of John Henry Cardinal Newman, chosen and edited by Charles Frederick Harrold. New York: Longmans, 1943.

HOGAN, MICHAEL, S.J. Newman and Bacon Bar God from Science. Jersey City: St. Peter's College Press, 1939.

JÖRIMANN, A. P. Exposé critique de la doctrine de Newman. Geneva: Henry Kündig, 1904.

JUERGENS, SYLVESTER P., S.M. Newman on the Psychology of Faith in the Individual. New York: Macmillan, 1928.

LAMM, WILLIAM R., S.M. The Spiritual Legacy of Newman. Milwaukee: Bruce, 1934.

LESLIE, SHANE. Studies in Sublime Failure. London: E. Benn, 1932.

LUNN, ARNOLD. Roman Converts. London: Chapman & Hall, 1924.

MAY, J. LEWIS. Cardinal Newman. London: Geoffrey
    Bles, 1929.

MEYNELL, WILFRED. Cardinal Newman. London:
    Burns & Oates, 1890. Fifth edition.

NÉDONCELLE, MAURICE. Cardinal John Henry New-
    man. Apologia pro Vita Sua, French translation
    by L. Michelin Delimoges. Introduction and notes
    by Maurice Nédoncelle. Paris: Bloud et Gay,
    1939.

NEWMAN, BERTRAM. Cardinal Newman: a biograph-
    ical and literary study. London: G. Bell & Sons,
    1925.

NEWMAN, FRANCIS. Contributions Chiefly to the Early
    History of the Late Cardinal Newman. Lon-
    don: Kegan Paul, Trench, Trübner & Co.,
    1891.

O'DWYER, EDWARD THOMAS. Cardinal Newman and
    the Encyclical Pascendi dominici gregis. London:
    Longmans, 1908.

PRZYWARA, ERICH, S.J. A Newman Synthesis. Lon-
    don: Sheed & Ward, 1932.

REINER, SISTER MARY ALOYSI, S.N.D. John Henry
    Newman, the Romantic, the Friend, the Leader.
    Boston: Collegiate Press Corporation, 1933.

RICKABY, JOSEPH, S.J. Index to the Works of John
    Henry Cardinal Newman. London: Longmans,
    1914.

SAROLEA, CHARLES. Cardinal Newman and His Influence on Religious Life and Thought. Edinburgh: T. & T. Clark, 1908.

THUREAU-DANGIN, PAUL. La renaissance catholique en Angleterre au XIX siècle. Paris: Librairie Plon, 1899–1906. 3 vols.

————. Newman Catholique d'après des documents nouveaux. Paris: Librairie Plon, 1912.

TOOHEY, JOHN J., S.J. An Indexed Synopsis of the "Grammar of Assent." New York: Longmans, 1906.

TRISTAM, H., and BACCHUS, F. "Newman" in Dictionnaire de théologie catholique. Paris: Letouzey et Ané, 1903–39.

WARD, WILFRID. Newman's Apologia pro Vita Sua. The two versions of 1864 and 1865, preceded by Newman's and Kingsley's pamphlets, with an introduction by Wilfrid Ward. London: Henry Frowde, Oxford University Press, 1913.

————. Last Lectures. London: Longmans, 1918.

WILLIAMS, W. J. Newman, Pascal, Loisy and the Catholic Church. London: Francis Griffiths, 1906.

WOODRUFF, DOUGLAS. "On Newman, Chesterton and Exorbitance" in For Hilaire Belloc, Essays in Honor of His 71st Birthday, edited by Douglas Woodruff. New York: Sheed & Ward, 1942.

SUPPLEMENTARY WORKS

ADLER, MORTIMER. How to Read a Book. New York: Simon & Schuster, 1940.

BAKER, A. E. Prophets for an Age of Doubt. London: The Centenary Press, 1934.

BARRY, WILLIAM. "The Oxford Movement" in The Catholic Encyclopedia. New York: The Universal Knowledge Foundation, 1907–12.

BUTLER, CUTHBERT, O.S.B. The Life and Times of Bishop Ullathorne. London: Burns, Oates & Washbourne, 1926.

CONWAY, BERTRAND L., C.S.P. The Question Box. New York: The Paulist Press, 1929.

DELANEY, SELDEN PEABODY. Why Rome. New York: The Dial Press, 1935.

HUTTON, W. H. "The Oxford Movement" in The Cambridge History of English Literature, edited by Sir A. W. Ward and A. R. Wallen, Vol. XII. Cambridge University Press, 1932.

Charles Kingsley: His Letters and Memories of His Life, edited by his wife. London: C. Kegan Paul & Co. Vol. I, fifteenth abridged edition, 1885; Vol. II, abridged edition, 1879.

LESLIE, SHANE. Henry Edward Manning, His Life and Labours. London: Burns, Oates & Washbourne, 1921. Second edition.

LUNN, ARNOLD. Now I See. New York: Sheed & Ward, 1934.

MAYNARD, THEODORE. Orestes Brownson, Yankee, Radical, Catholic. New York: Macmillan, 1943.

O'BRIEN, JOHN A. The Faith of Millions. Huntington, Ind.: Our Sunday Visitor Press, 1938.

PURCELL, EDMUND SHERIDAN. Life of Cardinal Manning. London: Macmillan, 1896. 2 vols.

STEDMAN, A. M. Oxford: Its Life and Schools. London: George Bell & Sons, 1887.

STRACHEY, LYTTON. Eminent Victorians. Garden City: Garden City Publishing Co. Undated.

Letters of Archbishop Ullathorne. London: Burns & Oates, 1892.

WALWORTH, CLARENCE E. The Oxford Movement in America, Glimpses of Life in an Anglican Seminary. New York: The Catholic Book Exchange, 1895.

WARD, MAISIE. Insurrection versus Resurrection. New York: Sheed & Ward, 1937.

WARD, MAISIE, and SHEED, F. J. Catholic Evidence Training Outlines. London: Sheed & Ward, 1939. Fourth edition.

WARD, WILFRID. William George Ward and the Catholic Revival. London: Macmillan, 1893.

WHALEN, DORAN. Granite for God's House, the Life of Orestes Augustus Brownson. New York: Sheed & Ward, 1941.

THEOLOGICAL BACKGROUND READING FOR THIS STUDY
CATHOLIC SOURCES

AQUINAS, ST. THOMAS. De veritate. Paris: Vivès, 1875.
Vol. XV.

BRUNHES, GABRIEL. Faith and Its Rational Justification, translated by Rev. W. A. Spence. London:
Sands & Co., 1931.

CHOSSAT, MARCEL, S. J. "Modernisme" in Dictionnaire
apologétique de la foi catholique. Paris: Gabriel
Beauchesne et Cie., 1911–22. Fourth edition.

FALCON, JOSEPH, S.M. La crédibilité du dogme catholique. Paris: Emmanuel Vitte, 1933.

FENTON, JOSEPH CLIFFORD. The Concept of Sacred
Theology. Milwaukee: Bruce, 1941.

FRANZELIN, IOANNIS BAPT. Tractatus de divina tra ›
ditione et Scriptura. Rome: Marietti, 1870.

GARDEIL, A., O.P. La crédibilité et l'apologétique.
Paris: Gabalda et Cie., 1912.

GRANDMAISON, LÉONCE DE, S.J. Le dogme chrétien.
Paris: Gabriel Beauchesne, 1927. Second edition.

HARENT, S. "Foi" in Dictionnaire de théologie catholique. Paris: Letouzey et Ané, 1903–39.

LAGRANGE, M. J., O.P. M. Loisy et le Modernisme.
Juvisy: Editions du Cerf, 1932.

LÉPICIER, ALEXIUS M. De stabilitate et progressu
dogmatis. Rome: Desclée, 1910.

MAHER, MICHAEL, S.J. Psychology, Empirical and

Rational. London: Longmans, 1908. Sixth edition.

MARIN-SOLA, F., O.P. L'évolution homogène du dogme catholique. Paris: J. Gabalda, 1924. Second edition. 2 vols.

PESCH, CHRISTIAN, S.J. Praelectiones dogmaticae. Friburg: Herder, 1910. Vol. XIII. Third edition.

PINARD DE LA BOULLAYE, H., S.J. L'étude comparée des religions. Paris: Beauchesne, 1925. 2 vols.

PIUS X. Encyclical, "Pascendi dominici gregis." Acta Sanctae Sedis, Vol. XL, 1907.

————. "Lamentabili sane exitu," decree of the Holy Office approved and confirmed by Pope Pius X. Acta Sanctae Sedis, Vol. XL, 1907.

————. "Letter to the Bishop of Limerick," approving his pamphlet on Newman's writings. Acta Sanctae Sedis, Vol. XLI, 1908.

RIVIÈRE, JEAN. Le Modernisme dans l'Eglise. Paris: Letouzey et Ané, 1929.

SCHULTES, R. M., O.P. Introductio in historiam dogmatum. Paris: Lethielleux, 1922.

TIXERONT, J. Histoire des dogmes. Paris: J. Gabalda et Fils, 1930. Twelfth edition. 3 vols.

VAN NOORT, G. Tractatus de fontibus revelationis necnon de fide divina. Bussum in Hollandia: Sumptibus Societatis Editricis Anonymae, 1920.

VERMEERSCH, A. "Modernism" in The Catholic Encyclopedia. New York: The Universal Knowledge Foundation, 1907–12.

NON-CATHOLIC SOURCES

Butler, Joseph. The Analogy of Religion Natural and Revealed to the Constitution and Course of Nature, with analytical preface and index by the Late Rt. Rev. Edward Steere. London: George Bell & Sons, 1886.

Church, R. W. Occasional Papers. London: Macmillan, 1897. 2 vols.

Fairbairn, A. M. The Place of Christ in Modern Theology. London: Hodder & Stoughton, 1898. Eighth edition.

Gladstone, William E. Studies Subsidiary to the Works of Bishop Butler. Oxford: Clarendon Press, 1896.

——. The Vatican Decrees in Their Bearing on Civil Allegiance. New York: D. Appleton & Co., 1874.

——. Vaticanism, an Answer to Reproofs and Replies. New York: Harper & Bros., 1875.

Loeppert, Adam J. Modernism and the Vatican, with an introduction by Bishop William F. McDowell. Cincinnati: Jennings & Graham. New York: Eaton & Mains, 1912.

Martineau, James. Essays Philosophical and Theological. London: Trübner & Co., 1869.

NEWMAN, FRANCIS WILLIAM. Phases of Faith; or, Passages from the History of My Creed. London: John Chapman, 1850.

PUSEY, E. B. An Eirenicon, in a Letter to the Author of "The Christian Year." New York: D. Appleton & Co., 1866.

SCHAFF, PHILIP. The Creeds of Christendom with a History and Critical Notes. New York: Harper & Bros., 1877. Fourth edition. 3 vols.

STEPHEN, LESLIE. An Agnostic's Apology. London: Smith, Elder & Co., 1893.

TUCKWELL, JAMES HENRY. Religion and Reality. London: Methuen & Co., 1915.

WORKS OF MODERNIST THEOLOGY AND VIEWPOINT

DIMNET, ERNEST. *La pensée catholique dans l'Angleterre contemporaine. Paris: Victor Lecoffre, 1906.

HOUTIN, ALBERT. *La question biblique chez les Catholiques de France au XIX siècle. Paris: Alphonse Picard et Fils, 1902. Second edition.

LEROY, EDOUARD. *Dogme et critique. Paris: Bloud et Cie., 1907.

LOISY, ALFRED. *Etudes évangéliques. Paris: Alphonse Picard et Fils, 1902.

————. *L'évangile et l'Eglise. Ceffonds, 1908. Fourth edition.

————. Simples réflexions sur le décret du Saint-

Office Lamentabili sane exitu et sur l'encyclique Pascendi dominici gregis. Ceffonds, 1908.

LOISY, ALFRED. Quelques lettres sur des questions actuelles et sur les évènements récents. Ceffonds, 1908.

———. *Mémoires pour servir à l'histoire religieuse de notre temps. Paris: Emile Nourry, 1930. 3 vols.

TYRRELL, GEORGE. The Faith of the Millions, first series. London: Longmans, 1901.

———. The Faith of the Millions, second series. London: Longmans, 1901.

———. Lex Orandi, or Prayer and Creed. London: Longmans, 1903.

———. Lex Credendi, a Sequel to Lex Orandi. London: Longmans, 1906.

———. A Much-Abused Letter. London: Longmans, 1906.

———. Through Scylla and Charybdis, or the Old Theology and the New. London: Longmans, 1907.

ARTICLES IN PERIODICALS AND REVIEWS

AVELING, FRANCIS. "Universals and the Illative Sense" in Dublin Review, Vol. CXXXVII (October, 1905).

BROWNSON, ORESTES A. " 'An Essay on the Development of Christian Doctrine' by John Henry Newman" (book review) in Brownson's Quarterly Review, Vol. III (1846).

————. " 'The Fourfold Difficulty of Anglicanism' by J. Spencer Northcote" (book review) in Brownson's Quarterly Review, Vol. I, new series (1847).

————. "Some Explanations Offered to Our Catholic Readers" in Brownson's Quarterly Review, Vol. I, national series (1864).

COTTER, A. C. "Alfred Loisy" in Theological Studies, May, 1941.

DIMNET, ERNEST. "Quelques aspects du Cardinal Newman" in Revue du clergé français, Vol. XXXIV, no. 201 (April 1, 1903).

GERRARD, THOMAS J. "Bergson, Newman and Aquinas" in The Catholic World, Vol. XCVI (March, 1913).

————. "The 'Grammar of Assent' and the 'Sure Future' " in Dublin Review, Vol. CXXXVII (July, 1905).

GRANDMAISON, LÉONCE DE, S.J. "John Henry Newman considéré comme maître" in Etudes, Vol. CX (January, 1907).

HARPER, THOMAS. "Dr. Newman's Essay in Aid of a Grammar of Assent" in The Month, Vol. XII (May and June, 1870); Vol. XIII (July and August, 1870).

————. "On Common Sense and Moral (in reference to Dr. Newman's Grammar of Assent)" in The Month, Vol. XIII (October, 1870).

————. "On Moral (in reference to Dr. Newman's

Grammar of Assent)" in The Month, Vol. XIII (November, 1870).

————. "Causation (in reference to Dr. Newman's Grammar of Assent)" in The Month, Vol. XIII (December, 1870).

HAYOT, MARCEL. "Brémond et Newman" in Revue apologétique, Vol. LXVII (November and December, 1938).

JUERGENS, SYLVESTER P., S.M. "What is Newman's Deepest Message?" in The Ecclesiastical Review, Vol. LXXVIII (1928).

LOISY, ALFRED. "Le développement chrétien d'après le Cardinal Newman" in Revue du clergé français, Vol. XVII (December, 1899). (Article signed "A. Firmin.")

————. "Les preuves et l'économie de la révélation" in Revue du clergé français, Vol. XXII (March, 1900). (Article signed "A. Firmin.")

REILLY, JOSEPH J. "Newman as a Controversialist" in The Catholic World, Vol. CXVII (June, 1923).

TREACY, JOSEPH V. "Newman as a Preacher" in American Catholic Quarterly Review, Vol. XVI (April, 1891).

TYNAN, MICHAEL. "The Approach to Newman" in The Irish Ecclesiastical Record, March, 1940.

WARD, WILLIAM GEORGE. "The Encyclical and Syllabus" in Dublin Review, new series, no. 7 (January, 1865).

————. "Extent of the Church's Infallibility—The Encyclical 'Mirari Vos' " in Dublin Review, new series, no. 8 (April, 1865).

Unsigned. "Cardinal Newman and Creative Theology" in Dublin Review, Vol. CXXXVIII (April, 1906).

Index

Achilli, Giacinto: sues Newman for libel, 14

"Additions" resulting from doctrinal development according to Newman, 96

Adler, Mortimer, 66 note

Ambrose, St., 32

An Agnostic's Apology by Leslie Stephen, 171 note

Analogia fidei, 74

Analogy of Religion by Bishop Butler, its effect on Newman, 8

Anglican works of Newman, 52 f.: reissued, 53 f.; their tone and spirit hardly Catholic, 54

Apologetics, Newman's works not substitute for, 21 ff.

Apologia pro vita sua
cited, 5 ff., 5 note, 24 f., 27 note, 32, 44, 118, 185 f., 189
controversial writing in first edition, 77
Loyola University Press edition, 45 note
new French edition, 117
Oxford University Press edition, 77
success of, 14 f.
referred to, 28 note, 40, 41 note, 73, 78

Apostles, their infused knowledge of dogma, 109 note

Apostles' Creed, 124

Arians of the Fourth Century, 10

Aristotle: Aristotelian *phronesis* and the Illative Sense, 167; not

Aristotle (*continued*)
in favor in Rome in 1846–47, 13 note

Assent
according to Newman, 160–66
in matters of religion, 162
"notional," 160 ff.
"real," 161
relation to inference, 162–66
simple, 163

Assent of faith according to Keble, 9

"Assimilation," meaning in Newman, 99 ff.

Atlantis magazine, 40 note

Autour d'un petit livre by Alfred Loisy, 181 note

Aveling, Francis, 196

Bacon, Lord, 49 f.

Bacon and Newman Bar God from Science by Hogan, 49 f., 67

Baker, A. E.: Newman called opponent of Liberalism, 28 note

Basil, St., 84

Belloc, Hilaire: on heroism demanded in Newman's conversion, 7; his description of English Church, 45 note

"Benedictine Schools," 40 note

Bergson, Henri, 194, 196

Blessed Virgin, 90, 197

Blessed Virgin, devotion to: defended by Newman, 45 f.; inculcated by Froude, 10

Bourdon, Hilaire, pseudonym of George Tyrrell, 148 note
Brémond, Henri, 171
British Critic magazine, 53 note, 100, 145
Brownson, Orestes: criticism of Newman, 97 ff.; misunderstanding of Newman's argument admitted by, 103 ff.
Brownson's Quarterly Review, cited, 97, 98 f., 100, 104
Butler, Bishop, 8, 179, 196
Butler, Cuthbert, 38 note, 57 note, 58 note

Cardinal Newman and the Encyclical Pascendi Dominici Gregis by O'Dwyer, 152 ff.
Cardinal Newman and William Froude, F.R.S., a Correspondence by Harper, 175 note
Cardinal Newman, His Place in Religion and in Literature by D'Cruz, 54 f., 160 note
Catholic Evidence Training Outlines by Maisie Ward and F. J. Sheed, 86 note
Catholic university in Ireland, Newman's difficulties with, 14
Catholic World, 62 note, 194 note
Charlemagne, 40 note
Chillingworth, 147 note
Chossat, Marcel: on Loisy's solution to problem of development, 125; on similarity between Newman and Loisy, 119
Church, Dean: on phases of Newman's religious progress, 5 f., 10
Church of Rome, Froude's admiration of, 10
Clement of Alexandria, 13 note
Collegio Romano, 92
Concept of Sacred Theology by Fenton, cited, 17 note

"Conditional proposition," meaning of the term in Newman, 66, 160
Conscience, Newman on freedom of, 58-62
Convergence of probabilities, argument from, 181-84
Conway, Bertrand L., 86 note
Copeland, W. J.: Newman's sermons republished by, 33 note
Corot, 159
Cotter, A. C., 124 note

Dalgairns, J. D., 13
D'Arcy, M. C., 160, 169, 199 note: on importance of *Grammar of Assent*, 170 note; on nature of Illative Sense, 166 note; on Newman's notion of universals, 196
D'Cruz, F. A., 160 note: on necessity of consulting Newman's Catholic works, 54 f.
De fontibus revelationis by Van Noort, 86 note
Delaney, Selden Peabody, 85 note
Delimoges, L. Michelin, 117 note
Depositum fidei, 138
De stabilitate et progressu dogmatis by Lépicier, 155 note
Development of Christian doctrine, theory of (*see also Essay on Development*)
development of implicit content to explicit, 94 ff., 107
differences between Newman's and Loisy's opinions on, 127 f.
and Loisy, 119-28
and Modernists, 112-54
postulation of initial deposit of revealed truth, 124 f.
Newman's originality in treating, 84 f.
Newman's ideas summarized, 86-91
and Tyrrell, 128-51

Difficulties of Anglicans: cited, 34 note, 38 f., 43, 45 f., 44 note, 58, 59 f., 95; referred to, 14, 31 note, 35 note

Dimnet, Ernest: admiration for Tyrrell, 148; article written in 1903, preference for University Sermon on development, 148 note; on Tyrrell, 128 and note

Discourses to Mixed Congregations, 14

Dogma
Loisy's idea of, 126
meaning of term in Newman, 94 ff.
Modernists' idea of, 114 f.
Newman's ambiguity on symbolic nature of, 147 note
Newman's idea of: not affected by his faulty conception of universals, 196 ff.
Tyrrell on symbolic nature of, 130

Douglas, Bishop, 34 note

Dublin Review, 14, 40, 41 and note, 196

Eclectic theory of religion not adopted by Newman, 102 f.

Eirenicon by Pusey, 34 note, 43

"The Encyclical and Syllabus," article in *Dublin Review* by Ward, 41 note

Engles, Ernest: pseudonym of Tyrrell, 148 note

English Catholic opposition to Newman, 14

English distaste for metaphysics, 44

English habits of belief and devotion, 43 f.

English mentality, 42-46

English sense of fair play, 45

Englishman's attachment to Established Church, 44 f.

Essay on Development (see also Development of Christian doctrine, theory of)
cited, 94 f., 98, 100 f., 110, 118 f., 121 ff., 135 ff.
cited by Tyrrell, 134
compared with University Sermon, 148 ff.
convenient link between two religious periods of Newman's life, 4 f.
criticisms from Catholic sources, 86, 92-105
criticisms from Protestant sources, 86, 106-11
criticized by Roman theologians, 92 ff.
definitive edition of 1878, 86 f., 99, 101, 147 and note
deposit of revelation supposed by, 139
differs from University Sermon on development, 140
first American edition, 98 note, 147 note
first edition, 87, 99, 101
and Keble's theory, 9
offered for revision, 118 f.
orthodoxy of, 93
praised by Modernists, 86
relation to Catholic apologetics, 22
summary of, 83-91
Tixeront on, 85 note
Tyrrell's view of, 131
referred to, 20, 56, 79, 106, 148 ff., 159, 201

Essays Critical and Historical, 53, 145 f.

Essays on Miracles, 9, 35 note, 53 note: development of Newman's thought, 11 and note

Essays Philosophical and Theological by Martineau, 106

Etudes, 178 note, 196

Etudes évangéliques by Loisy, 125 note

Exegesis preferred to doctrine in Roman schools, 13 note

Existence of God, traditional proofs of, 172 f., 177 ff.

"Extent of the Church's Infallibility—The Encyclical 'Mirari Vos,'" article in *Dublin Review* by Ward, 41 note

"Extremist School" criticized by Newman, 37-42

Faber, criticized by Newman, 38 f.

Fairbairn, A. M.: criticism of *Essay on Development*, 107-11

Faith of Millions by O'Brien, 86 note

Falcon, Joseph, 182 note

Fathers of Church, 33 f., 146

Fenton, Joseph Clifford, 17 f.

Firmin, A.: pseudonym of Loisy, 120

Folghera, J. D., ix note

For Hilaire Belloc, edited by Woodruff, 28

Franzelin, 96 note, 109 note

Friedel, Francis J., 96 note

Froude, Hurrell, 10, 44 note

Froude, Mrs. William, 150

Froude, William, 175, 176 note

Gerrard, Thomas J., 16 note, 194

Gladstone, William E., 58, 61: on decrees of Vatican Council, 31, 57

Grammar of Assent
cited, 32, 147 note
contribution to theological literature, 198 f.
and Keble's theory, 9
and Modernists, 180-91
and objective religious truth, 169-79
positive value of, 192-99
relation to Catholic apologetics, 21

Grammar of Assent (continued)
summary of, 157-68
referred to, 14, 20, 56, 63, 66, 79, 83, 201

Grandmaison, Léonce de, 85, 96 note, 120 note: criticisms of Newman, 178, 196

Granite for God's House by Whalen, 97 note

Gregory Nazianzen, St., 84

Guitton, Jean: on "idea" in Newman, 137

Harent, S., 181 note, 182 note, 185 note

Harper, Gordon Huntington, 175 note

Hermes, 94

Histoire des dogmes by Tixeront, 85 note

Historical Sketches, 40 note

Hogan, Michael, 69 note: on Newman's view of science, 49 f., 67 ff.

Holy See, 113: Newman's obedience to, 118

Homer, 200

Hope-Scott, James R., 13

Houtin, 148 note, 180, 181 note, 185

How to Read a Book, by Adler, 66 note

Hume, 196

Husslein, Joseph: on Newman's sermons, 62 f.

Hutton, W. H.: on Newman as the parent of Modernism, ix note

"Idea": distinguished from its object in Newman, 136 ff.; meaning of the term in Newman, 110, 135-38; Newman's meaning of "aspect" of, 135-38; Tyrrell's interpretation of Newman's meaning of, 134-38

Idea of a University, 14, 20 note: Father Hogan's criticism of, 49 f., 67 ff.

Illative Sense, 184: an intellectual function, 193; meaning of the term in Newman, 166 ff.

Immaculate Conception, 117: defended by Newman, 34 f.

Index to the Works of John Henry Cardinal Newman by Rickaby, 77

Infallibility, 30 f., 108 ff.

Inspiration, Newman on, 200

"Institution," meaning of the term in Newman, 109 f.

Insurrection versus Resurrection by Maisie Ward, 154 note

Introductio in historiam dogmatum by Schultes, 154 note

Irenaeus, St., 84

Jarrett, Bede: on Newman as a theologian, viii f.

Jerome, St., 84

John, St., 95

Juergens, Sylvester P., 10 note, 29 note, 158, 193: on Liberals, 159 note; on Newman's purpose in writing *Grammar of Assent*, 176 f.

Keble, John: influence on Newman, 9

Kingsley, Charles, 77

La crédibilité du dogme catholique by Falcon, 182 note

Lagrange, M. J., on Loisy, 116 note

Lamentabili sane exitu, 180, 184 f., 191 f.

Lamm, William R., 63 note

La pensée catholique dans l'Angleterre contemporaine by Dimnet, 128 note: placed on *Index*, 148 note

La philosophie de Newman by Guitton, 137 note

Lectures on Justification, 10

Le dogme chrétien by Grandmaison, 85, 96 note, 120 note

Le Modernisme dans l'Eglise by Rivière, 116 note

Leo XIII, 156

Lépicier, Alexius M., 155 note

Le Roy, 148 note

Letter to Dr. Pusey, 33 f., 38 f., 43

Letter to the Duke of Norfolk, 31 note, 57 ff.

Letters and Correspondence of John Henry Newman, edited by Anne Mozley, 169 note

L'étude comparée des religions by La Boullaye, 181 note

L'évangile et L'église by Loisy, 119 note, 128 note

L'évolution homogène du dogme catholique by Marin-Sola, 84 f., 96 note, 154 note

Lex Credendi by Tyrrell, 129 f.

Lex Orandi by Tyrrell, 129

Liberalism in religion: Newman alive to dangers of, 39; Newman's definition of, 27 note; Newman's opposition to, 18, 27 f., 40, 74

Life and Times of Bishop Ullathorne by Butler, 38 note, 57 note, 58 note

Life of Cardinal Manning by Purcell, 31 note, 37

Life of John Henry Cardinal Newman by Wilfrid Ward: cited, x, 6, 13, 15, 19 note, 28 and note, 52, 53 note, 92 f., 177; most authoritative biography, 76; referred to, 8, 38 note, 40 note, 42 note, 57 note, 70, 160 note

Locke, 158 f., 163, 196

Loisy, Alfred called "disciple" of Newman, 116 f.

Loisy, Alfred (*continued*)
  and development, theory of, 119-28: applies theory of development to Old and New Testaments, 128; confuses Christianity itself with its development, 125; exaggerates Newman's theory of development, 120-24; summary of relationship between his theory and Newman's, 127 f.
  dogma: his idea of, 126; his theory derogatory to dogmatic formulas of Church, 123; "transformation" of dogma taught by, 121 f.
  natural and supernatural certitudes confused by, 187 ff.
  probabilities: could not lead to certitude, according to, 191; Newman's theory misrepresented by, 185-91
  religious ideas in 1894, 123 f.
  sacraments, efficacy attacked by, 128
  works among sources of doctrines condemned by *Pascendi*, 113
Loss and Gain, 20 note
Lunn, Arnold: impressed by *Essay on Development*, 85 note; on relationship between faith and reason in Newman, 16 f.

Maher, Michael, 169 f.
Manning, Cardinal, 37: eulogy of Newman delivered by, 15; Newman's disagreement with policies of, 14, 39 f.
Marin-Sola, 84 f., 96 note, 154 note
Mariology of Cardinal Newman by Friedel, 96 note
Martineau, James, 111: criticizes *Essay on Development*, 106 f.
Maynard, Theodore, 97 note
Mémoires pour servir à l'histoire

Mémoires (*continued*)
  religieuse de nôtre temps by Loisy, 119, 128 note, 181 note
Meynell, Dr., 173
Middle Ages, theological speculation in, 40 f.
Modernists, 72
  attempt to use *Essay on Development*, 19
  Newman not guilty of their heresy, 117 ff.
  Newman's teachings misrepresented by, 65
  praise *Essay on Development*, 86
  summary of their position not clearly presented by, 112
  their teachings summarized in *Pascendi*, 112-19
  their unorthodoxy not clearly exposed in their writings, 124
  undermine foundations of Catholic doctrine, 112
M. Loisy et le Modernisme by M. J. Lagrange, 116

The Nature of Belief by M. C. D'Arcy: cited, 166 note, 170 note, 196; referred to, 160, 199 note
Nédoncelle, Maurice, 117 note
"New apologetics": in disrepute among better modern theologians, 21; Newman called father of, 20 f.
Newman, Francis W.: brother of the Cardinal, 79
Newman, John Henry Cardinal
  biographical notes on, 3-15
  cardinalate, 15
  classification of his works, 19 f.
  "concealed Romanist" charge denied by, 5 note
  development of his religious thought, 5-13
  division of his life, important to

Newman, John H. (*continued*)
students of his theology, 52-55
fundamental principles of his idea of religion, 24-29, 71-74
his arguments difficult to summarize in form, 67-70
his sense of humor, 35 f.
intellectual honesty of, 38-42
language, his precision of, 64
literary style of, vii f.
quest for true Church satisfied with his conversion, 12
reception into Church, effect on theological thought of, 12 f.
renounced idea that Catholic Church is bound up with cause of Antichrist, 25 note
Roman study produced no great effect on his manner of writing, 13
theologian: his method as, 30-36; his place as, 16-23; not a Molinist or Scotist, 16; not a scholastic, 16, 18 f., 23; not a systematic, viii, 19, 22; not a Thomistic, 16
sincerity in matters of religion, 5 ff.
spiritual element in his writings, 36
technical phraseology avoided by, 19 note
temperament of, 37-46
"Newman as a Controversialist," article in *The Catholic World* by Joseph J. Reilly, 61 f.
Newman as a Man of Letters by Joseph J. Reilly, 62 note
Newman.—Essai de biographie psychologique by Henri Brémond, 171
Newman on the Psychology of Faith by Juergens: cited, 158, 159 note, 176 f., 193; referred to, 10 note, 29 note

Newman's Apologetic by Folghera, ix note, 29 note
Norfolk, Duke of, 58
Northcote, J. Spencer, 97 note
Now I See by Arnold Lunn, 85

O'Brien, John A.: approves Newman's theory of development, 86 note
O'Dwyer, Edward Thomas, 155: defends *Essay on Development*, 152 ff.
Oratory of St. Philip Neri, founded in England by Newman, 14
Orestes Brownson, Yankee, Radical, Catholic by Theodore Maynard, 97 note
Origen, 84
Oxford University Sermons, 9 f., 53 note, 171
belief: Newman's theory tentatively outlined in, 157; problem treated in, 173
sermon on "The Theory of Developments in Religious Doctrine": cited, 139 note, 140-43; considered by Tyrrell as on side of "liberal" theologians, 131; differs from *Essay on Development*, 140; *Essay on Development* must be preferred to it as definitive expression of Newman's thought, 148 ff.; interpreted by Tyrrell, 134-38; foundation for claim that Newman held symbolist view of dogma, 140-45; regarded by Tyrrell as more truly representative of Newman's theory than the *Essay on Development*, 138; seems dangerously close to philosophical idealism, 141 ff.; significant omissions when cited in *Essay on Development*, 147 and note; supposes

Oxford Sermons (*continued*)
original deposit of revealed truth, 139 note; tentative and hypothetical tone of, 143 f.; tentative expression of theory of development, 20, 77, 83; why not annotated in later editions, 146 note

Parochial and Plain Sermons, 10, 53 note, 72

Pascendi dominici gregis, 152 ff.: condemns Modernism, 113; summarizes Modernist teachings, 113-119

Paul, St., 95

Perrone, 70, 93 f., 150

Pesch, Christian, 184

Petavius, 33

Pinard de la Boullaye, H., 181 note

Pius X, 113, 181 note: letter to Bishop O'Dwyer in praise of Newman, 155 f.

Place of Christ in Modern Theology by Fairbairn, 107 f.

Pontius Pilate, 124

Praelectiones dogmaticae by Pesch, 184

Present Position of Catholics in England, 14, 36 and note

Principles of interpretation of Newman's works, 47-74:
and criticisms of Newman, 79
first principle, 52-55: application to *Essay on Development*, 99, 103; application to *Grammar of Assent*, 158; application to Loisy's interpretation of Newman's argument from probabilities, 185-89; how to use, 76; stated, 55; and Tyrrell's criticism, 151
second principle, 56-63: application to *Essay on Development*, 101, 103; application to *Grammar of Assent*, 172-79; application to Loisy's inter-

Principles (*continued*)
pretation of Newman's argument from probabilities, 189 f.; falsely used by Tyrrell, 138-51; how to use, 77 f.; stated, 63
third principle, 64-70: application to Tyrrell's criticism of *Essay on Development*, 138, 151; how to use, 78; stated, 70
fourth principle, 71-74: how to use, 78 f.; stated, 74
necessity of, 47-51

Probabilities: argument from convergence of, 181-84; meaning in Newman, 93 f., 182 note

Probability the guide of life, 164

Probable argument, its meaning in Newman, 93 f.

Propaganda College in Rome, 150

Prophetical Office, 70

Prophets for an Age of Doubt by A. E. Baker, 28 note

Protestant criticisms of *Essay on Development*, 86, 106-11

Protestants, 72

Psychology, Empirical and Rational by Michael Maher, 169 f.

Purcell, E. S., 31 note, 37

Pusey, E. B., devotional practices on Continent condemned by, 43

Quelques Lettres sur des questions actuelles et sur des événements récents by Alfred Loisy, 126 note

Question biblique au XXe siècle by Houtin, 181 note

Question Box, by Conway, 86 note

Reading, elementary rules of, 48 f.

Real Presence, doctrine upheld by Hurrell Froude, 10

Reason in theology, Newman's views on, 17

Reformation, Hurrell Froude's dislike for, 10

Reilly, Joseph J., 61 f.

Religion: eclectic theory not adopted by Newman, 102 f.; Newman's idea of fundamental principles of, 24-29, 71-74; origin of religion according to Modernists, 114; Tyrrell's notion of, 129 f.

Religion and Reality by Tuckwell, 25 f., 27 note

Religious thought, foundations of Newman's, 24-29

Revelation, Tyrrell's notion of, 129 f., 133 f.

Revised editions of Newman's works, necessity of consulting, 76

Revue du clergé français, 120 ff., 128 note, 148 note, 181 note, 185, 187 note, 190 ff.

Rickaby, Joseph, 77

Rivière, Jean: on Tyrrell, 116 note

Sacramental system taught by Keble, 9

Sacred Congregation of the Holy Office condemns Modernism, 113, 180

Sarolea, Charles, 172: evaluation of Newman's theology, ix; on influence of Newman, 47 f.

Scholastic phraseology not used by Newman, 13

Schultes, 154 note

Science and God, according to Newman, 50

Science, physical: its "atheism" according to Newman, 67 ff.

Select Treatises of St. Athanasius, 10

Sheed, F. J., 86 note

Simples réflexions sur le decret du Saint-Office Lamentabili sane exitu et sur l'encyclique Pascendi dominici gregis by

Simples réflexions (continued) Loisy, 113 note, 119, 181, 191 note

Speculation: Newman avoided elaborate, 32; Newman did not believe in suppression of, 40 f.

Spiritual Legacy of Newman by William R. Lamm, 63 note

Stade, 129 note

Stephen, Leslie, 171 note

Stromata of Clement of Alexandria used in Rome in 1846-47, 13 note

Talbot, George: criticizes *Letter to Pusey*, 37; influence against Newman, 14

Terminology, Newman's, 92-96, 193

Theology: nature of, 17 note; Newman's (*see* Newman, John Henry Cardinal: theologian); Tyrrell's notion of, 129-33

Thomas Aquinas, St.
admitted development of implicit content of revelation to explicit, 84
lack of influence on Newman, 16
mentioned in Newman's writings, 16 note
not in favor in Roman Schools in 1846-47, 13 note
on obligation of conscience, 60 note
relationship of his teaching to Newman's, 194 and note
seems to reject Immaculate Conception, 117

Through Scylla and Charybdis by Tyrrell, cited, 129, 131-34, 138, 144, 145 note

Thureau-Dangin, Paul, 38 note, 57 note

Timothy, 95

Tixeront, J., 85
Tract 71, 32
Tractarians, 138, 149
Tractatus de divina traditione et scriptura by Franzelin, 96 note, 109 note
Tuckwell, J. H., 25 f.: finds Newman useless as religious guide, 26
Tynan, Rev. Michael, 3, 43
Tyrrell, George
  admired by Dimnet, 148 note
  called "disciple" of Newman, 116 f.
  influenced by Newman, according to M. Nédoncelle, 117
  logical spokesman for Modernists, 116
  maintains Newman attached to "liberal" school in theology, 133
  Newman's theory of development not adopted by, 128 f.
  "old" and "new" theology, his notions of, 131-33
  relationship between theology and revelation, according to, 129 f.
  religion, his notion of, 129 f.
  revelation, his notion of, 129 f., 133 f.
  symbolic nature of dogma, according to, 130
  theory of development, his notion of, 128-51
  works of, among sources of doctrines condemned by *Pascendi*, according to Loisy, 113

Universal idea, Newman's conception of dogma not vitiated by his notion of, 195 ff.

Van Noort, 96 note
Vatican Council, 42, 57, 109
Vatican Council Decrees in Their Bearing on Civil Allegiance by W. E. Gladstone, 31 note
Vaticanism: an Answer to Reproofs and Replies by W. E. Gladstone, 58, 61
Via Media, 95
Victoria, Queen, 46
Vincent of Lerins, 84
Von Hügel, F., 117

Walsh, James J., 50
Ward, Maisie, 86 note, 154 note
Ward, Wilfrid, 13, 15, 19 note, 28 note, 38 note, 40 note, 42 and note, 53 note, 57 note, 70, 76, 92, 93, 160 note, 177
Ward, William George, 30 f.: criticized by Newman, 38 ff.; his dogmatism distasteful to Newman, 41; opposition to Newman, 14; theologian, 41 note
Whalen, Doran, 97 note
Whately, 28 note
White, Blanco, 28 note
Why Rome by S. P. Delaney, 85
Woodruff, Douglas: calls Newman greatest enemy of modern Liberalism, 28